SIMPLE TRUTHS

The Book

A Spiritual Guide For Mankind's Awakening

Cover Design: T&H Graphics

Interior Layout: T&H Graphics

ISBN: 978-0692607459
      0692607455

Library of Congress Control Number: 2016905317

CreateSpace Independent Publishing Platform, North Charleston, SC

This book is dedicated in loving memory of

Andrew Dale Royal

my little brother

(Andy)

8.18.67 ~ 3.18.16

ACKNOWLEDGMENT

I would like to express my gratitude to my mother for bringing me into this world and to my father and grandfather for their genetic gifts given to me along with the spiritual and moral foundation instilled in me by their words and actions. I am also grateful for the love and support I have received throughout my life from my two sisters, Stevie and Jan, and the countless lessons I have learned and the spiritual growth received from my little brother, Andy.

I am eternally grateful to God for being chosen to bring forth the wisdom within this book, which was given to me intuitively. I acknowledge that though it comes from my hand, the brilliance within these pages originates with God, and I am only a humble servant of the process.

I would like to express my gratitude to Jacqueline (Jackie) Jolley for her tireless devotion, taking on a stack of handwritten words and overseeing the evolution of this book into the finished work you hold in your hands. I am also grateful for Jackie's husband, Curtis Jolley, for all the free help and his eternally positive energy. I would like to thank David Ferris, the editor of this book, for his editorial magic and guidance. You are all Heaven-sent.

God's hands have been on this book from the very beginning, guiding the timing and direction of the project in ways that boggle the mind. Everyone whom God has guided to this project has been affected in a positive manner, adding light and an understanding that they can apply in their lives.

I don't have words to express the spiritual growth and blessings I have received in the eleven years spent writing this book. I know from experience what the wisdom in these words can do for you. I am excited for you and dedicate this book to you, my brothers and sisters.

FOREWORD

We are living in an incredible time in our evolution as children of God, a time of spiritual enlightenment on a deep, conscious level, awakening those who are ready to move into a more intuitive, receptive relationship with God, each other, and creation.

God's cosmic engine that animates the universe, planets, and us is moving the energy that supports our Adventure here on planet earth away from the self-centered outward energy toward a greater self-awareness. We are moving back towards the light of God and a golden age of conscious oneness with God and each other. The natural disasters and social upheavals that are occurring more frequently now are the effects this energy shift is having on mother earth and mankind. We have entered a phase where the self-centered structure that we have been creating is no longer supported by the creative force (God) and is now moving us into a more intuitive receptive phase.

This book is written for the more selfless among us who will have access to the greatest power and wisdom and will lead our movement into this next golden age. As challenging as this time is in our evolution as children of God, we have been given all the necessary ingredients and are being supported on a conscious level in ways that will ensure our success. Our greatness already lies within us.

This book is given to assist us in unlocking our true potential as children of God. Each of us is a piece of the puzzle that makes up this grand picture of perfection. And as time marches us into the golden age awaiting us, many are awakening to their true nature and their role in this great Adventure. Having access to the wisdom that animates creation will bring new meaning to life and elevate our conscious energy to a higher, more productive level.

The wisdom in this simple book has been available throughout the ages and has in these pages been articulated in a way that places that understanding and mastery within our grasp. All that is required is our desire.

SIMPLE TRUTHS - TABLE OF CONTENTS

WHO WE ARE

WHY ARE WE HERE

DYNAMICS OF CREATION

Who We Are

1

SIMPLE TRUTHS

Who are you and what is your purpose for being? Who or what is God, and what is your relationship to God? Where is God, and how can you find him or her? With all the time we have invested in our search for Truth, it seems that these Simple Truths should not be so elusive. Could it be that the Truth is right under our noses and we just haven't looked? Jesus said that the Kingdom of Heaven is right here, right now; it always has been and always will be. Muhammad said that God is as close as your jugular. The Truth is that God is within you and you are within God. You and God are One and God is greater.

Getting to the Simple Truth about who we are is pretty straightforward once we stop looking outside of ourselves and begin looking within. Think about God being separate from us and us being separate from God as long and hard as you like; the math doesn't add up if God the Creator is separate from us the Created. The synchronistic dance, the interconnectedness of All that is would be impossible to create and maintain if the Creator were separate from the Creation. We and God are one, consciously connected, and it is our connection to that greater All-encompassing power (God) that gives us the energy we express, and the guidance to express it.

You will be mesmerized when you take an honest look at how we see ourselves and God, how we have allowed centuries of misinformation to obscure the Simple Truth about what God and our true nature are and how we are connected consciously. As you awaken to your true state of consciousness and begin to look within, you will be amazed by having lived for so long under such an obvious untruth as that which we are living under. Even if our present reality is uncomfortable, it is familiar, it is what we have decided we know, and letting go of the familiar can be frightening. It takes courage to let go of the very substance that your reality is based upon.

But how is your reality working for you? If you think life is great, and you have no doubts that you are headed in the right direction, this book might not be for you. If you sense that there is something greater than you, that seems to be just beyond your grasp, that you can't see with your eyes yet you know is there, you can't touch with your hands, but you feel it, you can't hear the words with your ears, yet you seem to know the song by heart – then open your heart, let go of all thoughts and feelings that don't abide in the realm of love, joy, and gratitude (Heaven), and prepare to meet the most beautiful, powerful person you will ever know: you!

The purpose of this simple book is to open you up to who you are, to give you the tools that will allow you to reconnect with the child of God that you are, remembering the unbreakable connection to God that has always been. It is God's Will that we grow into all the glory that is God. Simply put, we are being touched by God – spiritually, emotionally, mentally, and physically. Our connection is never broken. When we don't feel this connection, it is because of the barriers that we create with our thoughts and feelings. Everything that is God's is already ours, it has always been ours, because we are God and God is greater. All the greatness, all the wisdom, all the power that is God is yours right now. All you have to do is clear away aspects of your thoughts and feelings that obscure this truth.

You have nothing to learn; you already know it. Your job is to simply let go of the thoughts and feelings that don't support your highest expression of self, reopening you to your true potential as an eternal, conscious being, clothed in your physical body, selflessly focused.

Jesus spent his life focused on his thoughts and feelings, balancing his thoughts and using his feelings to verify that his thoughts were correct. Jesus knew that any thoughts that caused him to feel discordant energy (to feel bad) worked against him. He knew to keep his attention in the moment (right here, right now), balancing his conscious energy and bringing it to its highest and most joyous expression. This is the gift Jesus gave us. The life he lived showed us that perfection is doable. He did it, he said we will do it and more, and Jesus didn't lie or exaggerate.

The question is right here, right now: are you ready to walk the path that Jesus walked back into oneness with God, to dwell in God's conscious light, to be one with God, and have all that is God's? This is God's gift to us as God's children. It is time to step forth and claim what is ours, to take our place as equals with God. It's God's Will that we succeed, and God has designed everything in this Adventure to guarantee our success. All we need to do is let go of our self-centered focus, start paying attention to our conscious energy (our thoughts and feelings), and learn to connect God's selfless conscious energy to our highest expression of self – what you could call a dance with God into a higher expression of self. The path is simple. God does all the heavy lifting; all we have to do is balance our thoughts and feelings and pay attention right here, right now, in the moment. Our thoughts and feelings will always give us the right answer if we listen.

Everything that is comes from consciousness. Consciousness became established as that first spark of energy that made self-evident that there was something to be aware of. Consciousness has two defined qualities: thought (masculine, outgoing, positive energy) and feeling (feminine, receptive, grounding energy). Both are vibrational energy that can be combined and manipulated, creating a myriad of different expressions of consciousness, both nonphysical and physical. Our purpose is to express our conscious energy, define that energy, and then refine it to its highest expression. That is what God does, and as children of God, created in God's conscious image, that is what we do. It is the purpose of this book to express the Simple Truth about who we are, and explain how to raise our consciousness to the vibrational level of Heaven, where God, and All that truly is, reside. All that is necessary is learning to let go of any thoughts and feelings that cause us to feel bad and don't serve our highest expression of self. This is done by realizing that our power does not lie in our past or in our future but right here, right now, and learning to live in the moment where God abides and creates All that is. It is in this moment that we find oneness with All that is, God.

Though at first glance this all may seem so abstract and theoretical, in fact this notion is elegant in its simplicity and straightforwardness. However, it does require desire, focus, and the ability to undergo the suffering that exercising aspects of self-centered focus creates. Becoming stronger, whether physically, mentally, emotionally, or spiritually, causes pain, but if this pain is wisely endured, it will eventually ease and leave one stronger in the end.

It is not easy, but it *is* doable. Jesus did it, and Jesus said we would do it. It is that simple.

2

G O D

Understanding God, and our relationship to God, seems difficult, if not impossible, when we view everything from a physical, self-centered point of view. We see God as a really big version of ourselves, when in truth we are personal versions of God, created in God's conscious image. The question, therefore, is "who is God and what is God's image?" If you look at God as a physical being that creates stuff separate from God, where does God get the raw materials to make every thing? What was God standing on when God created every thing? And who created God?

There are too many questions that just can't be answered by viewing God as a physical, finite being. So what if God really is no thing? What is no thing? Is it light? No! Light is some thing. Is it dark? No, dark is some thing! Is it emptiness? No, to be empty, there must be some *thing* to be empty. Think about this. God is no thing, but what is no thing? If it isn't some thing, how can we physical beings know it and how in God's name can we be created in its image if God is no thing and we are some thing? Do the math. With God being no thing and us being some thing, you can't get a logical answer, and God is logic. With these apparent dichotomies, a logical answer seems forever out of reach.

The answer is relative. The state of no thingness, where God comes from and always returns to, is a subjective state of being (consciousness), a state of pure awareness. Consciousness is no thing: it can't be seen or touched physically, yet every thing that is, comes from and is maintained by consciousness (no thing). God is pure potential, pure potential to be any thing and every thing, limited only by God's awareness of God. God's purpose for being is to know God, and God being every thing that is, wants to know everything about God.

Being all that is has certain limitations. If God is all there is, then

God has to create every thing that is, from light to lead and every thing in between, from no thing (pure consciousness). God has had to discover the dynamics of consciousness, separating thought from feeling and then re-blending the two in order to create the myriad of stuff that God uses, in order to define God. God's purpose for being is to be more aware, to express God, define God, and then refine the defined expression to its highest vibrational level.

It is God's subjective state of awareness (God's unwavering view of the desire fulfilled) that creates the matrix (blueprint) that supports and animates this physical, objective Adventure. What is seen as our physical, three-dimensional realm is simply an objective manifestation that we (God) use to advance our understanding of ourselves (God). The Adventure that we are experiencing with God's eternal support is what God experienced with God's eternal support. Yes, just like us, God has a family tree, a conscious family tree that transcends time and space. With all of God's countless lives, with a myriad of defined conscious points of focus, God is one consciousness with depth and diverse levels of awareness. God is truly omnipotent and omnipresent.

It was necessary for us, just as God did, to come into this phase of our evolution, forgetful of our true nature as pure selfless consciousness. What we are experiencing, God has experienced countless times before, because we and God are one and God is greater. Just like our physical family tree allows each generation to stand on the conscious foundation of the generation before it and reach higher toward understanding and perfection, our eternal conscious evolution as God is based on the same incredible principle of truth. Not only are you and God one, but your connection to All that is (God) gives you access to All that is, literally! All the miracles that Jesus and all evolved masters have ever performed, including the Resurrection and Ascension of Jesus, were done using this sacred conscious connection with God.

God had to experience what we call the Fall from the childlike state of selfless oneness with All that is, just like us. God had to experience the sense of being separate in order to gain God's I Am. The experience, as painful as it is, is the most effective way to achieve conscious understanding and bring it to its highest vibrational level (perfection).

Knowing that God is every thing and that everyone is a conscious point of God's omnipotent, omnipresent awareness helps one to understand that truth that Jesus spoke: "What you do to the least of my brothers, you do unto me." This statement speaks of God's omnipresence, our conscious connection to this presence, and our conscious connection to each other. Pretty powerful statement, don't you think?

What is important is that to understand God, you have to know yourself. To know yourself, you have to understand God. You can't know one without knowing the other because it is all the same thing – God. You and God are one, and God is greater. Knowing ourselves and knowing God are one and the same. Knowing yourself and knowing God is always an inward journey; it is a personal relationship with selfless awareness. If you truly wish to understand everything out there in the world, and the dynamic conscious energy behind it, go within, get quiet, and begin the most powerful and loving relationship you will ever have — knowing yourself and God. Knock and God will answer. It is God's law, and God cannot fail you. The simple truth: God is consciousness, and our connection to God is conscious (thought and feeling).

Until we realize this, and stop seeking a physical being that is separate from us in our pursuit of spiritual fulfillment, we will live under the illusion of physical separation. But as we learn to take the time, quiet ourselves, and listen to our thoughts and feelings, our focus will begin to shift from a self-centered state of separation back into a selflessly centered oneness with All that is, God. Our awareness shifts from love of self (our and God's I Am) back to God's selfless love with a conscious connection to All that is: God!

3

M A N

Who are we, what is our purpose for being, and what is our relationship to God? We are children of God, and our purpose for being is to bring God's eternal understanding to its highest vibrational expression, building on the conscious foundation of understanding that God has established on God's eternal quest for understanding. Our relationship to God is conscious. Each and every one of us is consciously connected to God via our thoughts and feelings. Think of your consciousness (thoughts and feelings) as a personal computer and God as the Internet. Your PC has the ability to compute a lot of information, but it is limited to what knowledge has been input into the computer. Yet if the operator of the computer knows how to access the Internet, all the wisdom that has ever been uploaded to the Internet is accessible.

The state of pre-Fall innocence in the Bible speaks to our selfless connection to All that is (God). We were part of the information of God's Internet, but we had no means of expression. We did not have our I Am (sense of self), our own personal terminal to express the incredible consciousness of which we were part. Our journey is to gain a personal, defined point of view, giving God's grand impersonal view a multitude of finely, very personal viewpoints of that truth. This is how God has become omnipotent, omnipresent, linking the impersonal mechanism of creation to a myriad of unique personal perspectives allowing for greater potential and growth.

The dysfunction in the world is the manifestation of our self-centered conscious energy that has not been balanced with God's all-knowing selfless awareness. The pain and separation we may feel, from God and each other, is also due to our imbalanced focus on our self-centered conscious energy without balancing it with God's selfless and loving conscious energy. By balancing selfless love (God's selfless all-knowing consciousness) with love of self (self-centered conscious focus necessary for developing our I Am), we exercise our consciousness, strengthening the aspects of self that elevate our thinking and feeling to a higher vibrational realm (Heaven), where we can unite with all of God's omnipotent and omnipresent consciousness. Access to God's realm of pure creative consciousness is always gained from within, consciously.

Remember that God is no thing (pure consciousness) and Heaven is no place. We will never find Heaven in the physical realm until we find Heaven within ourselves consciously. Once we find Heaven within our consciousness, we understand that it is a state of being, and we can live in the conscious state of Heaven even while standing in poop. The way to gain access to Heaven is by learning to eliminate negative thoughts and feelings. When we feel negative thoughts and feelings, we tend to pull them close and make them very personal, bringing our focus in on ourselves, and the pain created by the discordant thoughts and feelings moves our focus away from that greater part of us and God. Instead, do the opposite: observe what these negative thoughts and feelings are doing to your physical body and your mental and emotional body. This simple practice draws your thoughts and feelings away from the self-centered realm of consciousness toward becoming an observer, raising your conscious vibrational energy into God's selfless realm of creativity (Heaven). Connecting to the greater creative conscious energy (God), which supports and inspires all creativity, requires a strong connection from you (your self-center) to the selfless creative force that binds and supports creation. Moving your attention away from the finite event causing the negativity you experience and focusing on how the energy within yourself is reacting to the experience allows you to raise the energy supporting the negative effects, raising you up above the lower energy into a higher realm of consciousness.

Everything of value is always created and maintained in this higher vibrational realm of Heaven. The vibrational realm of Heaven is reached by entertaining positive thoughts and feelings; love, gratitude, and joy is the best way to get to Heaven. Hatred, anger, and grief are an expressway to Hell. Just like Heaven, Hell is not a physical location but a state of being. We can be standing in Disneyland and be in a state of Hell. Heaven and Hell are no place, but they are always a thought and feeling away. We are Creators, created in God's conscious image. Think about this: as we are, God once was; as God is, we will be.

You are a Creator. What are you creating for yourself and the people in your life? Do you spend more time in Heaven or Hell? As a child of God, much has been given to you. As a child of God, much is expected of you. If we are to inherit all that is God's, we first must become the responsible, mature children of God that we are meant to be. We do this one thought and feeling at a time. Letting go of self-centered, negative, conscious energy that doesn't serve our highest expression allows our true nature to shine forth, illuminating every aspect of our lives and allowing us to walk consciously with God.

4

W H O   Y O U   A R E

We are children of God, created in God's image, but what is that? Many see God created in our image: a grey-haired old man who is very wise and very loving but who tends to get pissed off and loses his temper from time to time. From that perspective, God does look much like us. But that is not the case. To understand God, ourselves, and our connection to God and All that is, we must know ourselves. We and God are infinite consciousness. What we see as reality is a finite expression of infinite consciousness, our physical bodies included.

This physical finite realm allows God and us to express, define, and refine infinite conscious energy in pursuit of understanding our full potential. God's immense experience has sufficiently broadened God's understanding such that we can create and then step into our creation and experience the effects of our creation as it evolves. That person you see in the mirror when you brush your teeth is the vehicle you chose to allow you to express, define, and refine your unique conscious energy at this time in your evolution as a child of God. The finite person you chose to be is as unique as you, the eternal infinite child of God that dwells within. The infinite you is the eternal part that transcends time and space and that chose your body at the time of its conception and will leave your physical body when this journey is completed.

You are an eternal being; think about this. To think that your eternal fate rests entirely on this one life is childish and small-minded. Look at the time spent living one life compared to the billions of years this universe has existed and will continue to exist, and understand that there have been countless Big Bangs, and there will be countless more. Now, imagine being you for eternity. As great as being you is, the eternal you will grow beyond your present state of understanding and will desire to express yourself in a new and improved manner, just as you have grown to your present point of understanding from prior lives lived. The person you chose to be in this life has all the right ingredients to allow you, the eternal child of God, to grow to your potential at this point in your eternal quest for understanding.

The finite part of who you are (your body) is an incredible means of expression that is unique unto itself. What you see as your family tree involves the transference of information from generation to generation, evolving with each generation and allowing for new attributes to be expressed. The moment of your conception in time and space gave you your unique expression of the information that came through your family tree. This blending of defined energy gives each and every one of us a very special connection to God, All that is, and each other. You are unique.

The Bible was written at a time when many lacked the ability to read and write. Information was conveyed from generation to generation by word of mouth, so a popular way of giving information became what is known as parables. Much of what can be found in ancient writings was written to convey complex information using stories that people of the time could understand, given their level of comprehension. Taking the stories like this literally will, in many cases, yield something other than the intended truth. Remembering this simple fact can be helpful when seeking information on your spiritual path to enlightenment.

It is said that we all come from Adam and Eve. This is true, but not in the finite sense of who we are. Our true infinite identity is one with God, each other, and All that is. We come from one singular consciousness. The story of Adam and Eve explains the formula involved in our creation (birth) and evolution. God starts with the whole of consciousness. That whole is separated into its two opposite forces, positively charged outgoing energy (Adam) and negatively charged receptive energy (Eve). The part about the rib explains the necessary process of injecting the desire for that which is to be objectified (created) with the feeling of the desire fulfilled. It is a two-way blending of thought and feeling, positive and negative and outgoing and receptive energy.

In the Garden of Eden, the snake represents growth (in order for a snake to grow, it must shed its skin or its outermost state), and the rib represents desire (God's desire to grow and expand God's omnipotent, omnipresent awareness). What has been left out of the story is Eve's contribution to the equation. First, Eve represents the receptive side of creation (consciousness), and to receive growth (knowledge) must enlist the outgoing positive side of conscious energy (Adam) to begin the process of creative dynamics.

Once Adam plucked the apple and shared it with Eve, an exchange of energy began that brought forth that which was desired. The formula is: first there is desire (this comes from the feminine, receptive side of consciousness), or Eve. This desire awakens Adam to what the desire is (pick the apple) and signals the relative dynamics of what is and what is not. It is the masculine outgoing thought (Adam) that is necessary to begin the process of embracing that which is to be understood and created. The positive outgoing energy of the thought (Adam) is then blended with the receptive grounding energy of intuition (Eve), which begins a creative exchange of conscious energy that is behind everything conscious, infinite and finite, from light to lead. It is the blending of this energy that is behind everything.

The binary code of our computer system is a simplified example of this dynamic. The ones represent the masculine outgoing positive side of creation and the zeros represent the feminine, intuitive receptive side of creation. Every process performed by your computer uses this formula, which is a simplified version of creation and made available by God to help us remember our creative powers and the dynamics involved in expressing ourselves as Creators.

Bottom line: you are created in God's image, infinite in nature. To know yourself you must go within, be still, and learn to listen to your flow of energy (thoughts and feelings). When your flow of energy is off-center, you feel it. As you become aware of your infinite flow of energy that connects the Me side of who you are with the We aspect of who you are, you begin to become aware of the truth that Jesus spoke – we and God are one, and God is greater. Understand that we can balance the energy that flows from that greater part of who we are (God) as it flows through us and returns back to that greater part (God), creating our unique conscious connection to God, each other, and All that is.

The inner pain and disease that we feel is the flow of energy grinding on the conscious clutter that accumulates from unprocessed thoughts and feelings (holding onto thoughts and feelings that don't serve our highest expression). The simple exercise of asking "How does this serve me?" allows us to eliminate this conscious clutter. The force is always with us and the freer it flows, the greater is our potential. We are all meant to be masters. Jesus was correct when he said that we would do the things he did, and greater. He lit the path that will lead each and every one of us to our greatest potential.

If you are having problems finding your light, look within. God put it in the last place many of us would think to look: right under our nose. Remember, God's light vibrates at a finer, higher rate and can't be seen. It must be felt. Pay attention!

5

T H E V E H I C L E

Who are you? It sounds like a simple question, but there's a lot of depth to who you truly are that many don't understand. This Adventure is a real hands-on experience that allows us to create and then stand in our creation and experience its effects. This Adventure can be painful at times, but the growth that is possible far outweighs the pain.

So, who are you? Breaking down the dynamics involved helps reveal the synchronistic complexity of the vehicle that is you. You are an eternal being created in God's image. You are conscious awareness, infinite and consciously connected to All that is (God). Being created in God's image, your purpose for being is growth, just like God. This Adventure is designed to allow you to express yourself in your own unique way, to define your specific conscious energy and refine that energy to its highest, purest expression.

That thing that you see when you look into the mirror is the vehicle that you chose as your means of expression in this life that you are living. Think of your body as a car. Each car is designed to serve a specific purpose, and each has distinct strengths and weaknesses. A Corvette is good on winding roads but isn't very good at hauling lumber. A minivan is great at moving the family around but makes for a poor road racer. Just as different vehicles possess certain characteristics that fulfill their respective purposes, the same is true with us. Our bodies give us a blending of strengths and challenges that allow for the relative dynamics that fuel our Adventure.

If you read the story of our beginning as children of God, we started as one. Of course, this story is not about our physical bodies. It is about us, our essence: pure conscious awareness. The Garden of Eden is a state of consciousness, not a physical state. Adam and Eve are not physical beings but are pure conscious awareness, yet to experience the physical realm. There had to be a means to allow for our interaction within this finite physical realm.

Much brilliance is involved in designing the vehicle that is you. There is your physical bloodline. In nature, everything knows its place and possesses a basic understanding of what to do and how to do it. Salmon know to swim upstream to breed, birds know to fly south, and bears know to take a nap in the winter. We come with a lot of information imprinted into the vehicle that is who we are. The saying, "The sins of the father are passed onto the son" speaks of the genetic information that gets passed from generation to generation. Each individual works within the genetic code that was imprinted upon them at the moment of their conception.

During our lives, we define and refine this conscious energy, which is imprinted upon the next generation. That is how evolution works, continually modifying the design of our physical bodies, but more importantly, the conscious evolution of our understanding as children of God. The moment in time and space of your conception gives you your unique alignment on the matrix that animates this Adventure. The alignment of energy is constantly moving and changing expression, ensuring that everything that comes into incarnation gets its own unique alignment to the matrix, (God's omnipotent, omnipresent energy) making everything unique with its own special connection to All that is (God).

Science can locate the precise position of the planets at any moment in time because of the precision of the matrix. At the moment of what science calls the Big Bang, the matrix that supports and guides what we see as reality was set in place. Likewise, the conscious energy that supports every possible scenario from the beginning of time to the end of time was set in place. Everything that comes into this realm comes with its own unique connection to this matrix.

Astrology is based on the understanding of the flow of energy and our unique connection to this energy. Our connection to the matrix does not make us perform in a predetermined manner but supplies us with our unique, constant flow of conscious energy that we continually express throughout our lives.

If you pay attention, you will notice that your inner conscious energy is continually changing in a relative manner. Our moods shift from good to not so good, our intellect moves between brilliance and dullness. Everyone feels the pull of this relative energy but few know to look to the energy that animates us to adjust the flow to a higher, finer expression. This can be accomplished by observing the energy that we feel in the moment that we are feeling it. Our creative power can always and only be accessed in the moment. Simply observing the flow of energy as it animates our lives allows us to understand the relative fluctuations enabling us to raise this energy to its higher vibrational expression, making for a lighter and more joyous life.

Many people are unaware that they are pure conscious energy clothed in physical bodies and are continually trying to push and pull their way through life in the physical realm, in opposition to the energy that supports their evolution. Once we realize this simple truth, we can start to work with the natural flow of energy as it unfolds instead of constantly struggling to rebalance ourselves to the energy we are not in sync with. Simply learning to take the time to be still and go within, to listen to what our thoughts and feelings are telling us, will put us in sync with the energy that connects us to God's omnipotent, omnipresent wisdom, giving us all the information we need to bring the moment to its highest expression. In doing so, our lives become more meaningful, a dance in perfect balance with God, and All that is.

6

THE BEGINNING

How do you reconcile an eternity that has always existed with the psychological need for there to be a beginning? Talk about a dichotomy! But our ingrained perspective gets in the way of the truth; we can't see the forest for the trees. How do you get some thing from no thing, and how can this some thing exist before it showed up? Figuring out what came first, the chicken or the egg, seems easy compared to this one.

Work it out logically, step by step. You're starting with no thing and from this no thingness, you need to get some thing. Enter relative dynamics! Creation comes from separating that which is to be created into its two opposite qualities. To get light, you must define the dynamics of what light is, from what it is not. It is dark that defines light and light that defines dark. To have "up" requires that there must be "down." You can't have beauty without ugly to define it, or sweet without bitter. This dynamic recurs in a myriad of ways throughout the universe.

The eternal infinite aspect of who we and God are is what has been referred to as the sacred feminine, selfless awareness, receptive in nature. That's half the equation that has always existed, transcending time and space, and existing in the eternal moment. Imagine being aware with no thing yet established to be aware of or receive. This is the eternal state that has always existed.

But what about the start? Was it God opening God's eyes, stretching and starting the day? This is where we must remember that all the information we see as this created realm was yet to be established. Eyes, arms, and day were yet to be created. As impressive as creation appears with all its larger than life expressions synchronistically dancing to and fro, God's beginnings were quite humble. It might help to think of the eternal half (sacred feminine) of the equation as a diaphragm or drum head. The beginning was initiated by vibration. Where did this vibration come from? The answer is relative dynamics. The eternal aspect of the equation has a defined quality or polarity much like the negative receptive side of a magnet. The start occurred when the natural flow was reversed in on itself. Simply put, God became self-aware. God realized "I am."

In the beginning the flow of energy was simple and has since consciously evolved to the reality we now perceive. As impressive as this all appears, at this point in our evolution as children of God, we are only aware of a small part of God's omnipotent, omnipresent abilities as Creator. Pay attention because we have moved into a phase where those of us who are ready are waking up and remembering our true nature as children of God created in God's conscious image.

7

PERSPECTIVE

If truth is self-evident, then how do you explain all the ignorance in the world? Why do we struggle to comprehend these simple truths when the explanation is all around us? It's a matter of perspective. We tend to forget that what we see as reality is an accumulation of information that has been established as our Adventure unfolds in time and space. When we are born, we come with a clean computer (our consciousness) imprinted with the basic structure that binds us to our role in this life but without all the information that we acquire over the course of our lifetime. The genetic code that is passed down from generation to generation, fine-tuned by the moment of our birth, gives each of us the basic structure (physical characteristics and personality traits) that allows us to express the defined conscious energy necessary to gain the specific understanding we have chosen to learn at this point in our evolution. Each life we live gives us this unique supportive structure that allows for a defined path in life, with a clean conscious mind, allowing for maximum growth.

Children learn and absorb new information more easily than adults because they have not yet cluttered their minds with contrary information that impedes the natural flow of conscious information. Remember that life is like a meal. We spend our days taking in experiences as we live, piling on conscious thought and feeling after conscious thought and feeling without investing the time to process the information. This process creates what is referred to as the veil, blocking the natural flow of conscious energy that connects us to each other, God, and All that is.

Our perspective tends to become that of the created, experiencing all the information that makes up our present reality without looking into the dynamics that supports our reality. Think of reality as a fountain of chocolate. The chocolate comes from deep within the depths of the fountain and is pumped up to the top, where it cascades down and returns to the depths of the fountain where it receives energy (heat), after which it is pumped back up to the surface again, allowing us to indulge in all that chocolate. How often do we think beyond where the strawberry meets the cascade of chocolate? We tend to keep our attention on the surface, rarely seeing beyond the strawberry and the chocolate.

The perspective of the Creator sees and understands the creative dynamics that began God's and our Adventure, and it is the relative exchange of infinite conscious energy that supports and energizes this physical finite world we live in. While the created stand on the surface of creation and must attempt to see through the complexity of All that has been created, the perspective of the Creator has access to the wisdom that was established in the very beginning when God realized "I am." Most people's view of reality is much like someone's limited understanding of a car. They know that you turn the key and the car starts, but they only have a vague idea of the complex mechanisms and interlinked technologies under the hood that propel the car forward.

Having the wisdom of the dynamics involved in creation can easily be applied to understand anything, allowing us to get to the core of what it is and what its purpose is without being overwhelmed with the complexity of information that appears on the surface. Life can be simple and fruitful, even on the most trying days, or it can be complex and burdensome. It all depends on our perspective.

8

T H E   B E A S T

Imagine you are God. You are omnipresent, you are omnipotent. You are all things. There is no thing that is not you. You are aware of all you create, and all you create is aware of you. That awareness of self has limitations. Total awareness of self is a selfless Adventure. Being aware of your All thingness, that you are All things, prevents you from having a self-centered (personal) awareness. How can you live with this awareness staring you straight in the eye all the time?

You need a means to experience God without being hindered by all of your selflessness. A way to take this awareness of the Creator and All that is and redirect it to an inward self-centered perspective of Creator walking amongst creation. To do so, God created what is called the Beast. God created competition — competition for food, competition for territory, competition for a mate, etc. This gave God's selfless conscious awareness its relative opposite, a self-centered point of reference. Each self-centered act created more information, allowing for greater separation from the eternal selfless state of awareness of All that is, giving more definition to both relative states. Over countless eons, God's eternal focus shifted from a selfless focus on the oneness of All that is to an inner focus, one based on a self-centered point of view, with the ability to experience creation not from the perspective of the Creator, but the exact opposite, the perspective of the created. Essentially, the act of God creating, climbing into that creation, and experiencing the effects of creation from both perspectives as Creator and created.

This change in focus allowed energy to gradually shift from a selfless awareness to a self-centered point of view. This energy has evolved throughout the whole animal kingdom, from single-cell amoebas to the most intelligent mammals. This energy evolved into what became Ego, the means for us (to Fall) into this Adventure of relative existence (God and Ego, good and evil). As we develop our sense of who we are as we live our lives, we define and strengthen our ego, giving us a stronger sense of self that comes from this separation from the greater selfless side of who we are (God). As we exercise aspects of self-centered energy that don't serve our highest interest, we begin to regain access to our true selfless energy, blending our personal self-awareness with the selfless awareness of All that is. This is the path that Jesus and all enlightened beings walk.

What Jesus was left with, once he exercised all aspects of self-centeredness that did not serve his highest expression of self, was perfect understanding of love, perfect understanding of joy: a perfect understanding of balance and its application in every moment of his life. Exercise adds strength to the structure of the physical body, or conscious mind, while eliminating useless weight that impedes the flow of energy and hinders freedom of movement. Having removed every untruth about his Ego gave Jesus the clarity of self necessary to regain his selfless identity as the Christ. We came from a state of knowing ourselves as God, and with that knowing had no personal identity. Our Fall has enabled us to acquire over many lifetimes our self-centered identity, and as we look at our actions in a non-judgmental way, we begin to see what works for us and what doesn't. As we begin to eliminate aspects of self-centered energy that don't serve us, we begin to remember our selflessness and our Godliness, our true connectedness to God.

With our new understanding of self, we comprehend love in all its vibrant glory because we now understand what love is not. We have the wisdom that comes from hurting and being hurt from the misdirected energy of love. We understand the pain caused by twisting and warping the selfless energy of love into self-centered desires to meet self-centered needs. We understand the dynamics of thought and feeling and begin to direct our conscious energy using this understanding.

This is the path that Jesus took; it is the path that all masters take, exercising all aspects of the Beast (self-centeredness) that obscure the selfless truth of who we are, Children of God. The simple act of observing the energy that animates our thoughts, feelings, and ultimately our actions, and balancing that energy, will yield the conscious clarity that Jesus and all true masters enjoy.

9

TAMING THE BEAST

Who are you and why are you here? It seems like a pretty simple question which should have a simple answer, yet many of us appear to be clueless. Could it be that we just aren't looking in the right place? Too many people see themselves only as physical beings, forgetting that they are eternal beings clothed in their physical bodies. We are created in God's image. The question is, what exactly is God's image? Many see God as a physical being. But if God were simply a physical being, where did God come from? Does God have parents? And, if so, where did *they* come from? There is no logical explanation to get to the truth about who we are. It is helpful to understand the simple dynamics of All that is, God.

First, how to reconcile how some thing (God) that has always existed came into being? The eternal part of who we and God are (remember, we and God are one and God is greater) is selfless. God has always been aware; that is the eternal part of what God is. The big question is at what point did something to be aware of come into being and how? Thinking in terms of time and space only confuses the issue. The trick is getting to the understanding that this thing we call reality is simply an expression of the truth, conscious awareness. Consciousness, what we perceive to be thought and feeling, is the infinite part of who and what we are. Time, space, and everything we see as being real are finite and an expression of our, and God's, conscious energy. This finite world is an expression of the infinite, conscious side of who and what we and God are. Our reality is a means for us, children of God, created in God's conscious image to express our conscious energy, define that energy, and refine it to its highest, purest expression. Consciousness, simply put, is the ability to receive information, process that information, and apply that information in a creative manner. Conscious energy is the relative interaction of that information (what it is vs. what it is not) being expressed. This Adventure we call life has been written by God and is being produced and directed by God, and all we have to do is express our own unique conscious energy within the defined conscious structure that came with our birth into this present life. God does not need anyone to step in and save the day or alter the story. God has it handled.

The moment in time and space of our conception, fine-tuned by the moment we enter this world at birth, gives us our own defined conscious matrix that guides and supports our Adventure. It is our responsibility to learn to still our thoughts and feelings and turn our attention inward to maintain our conscious connection to God, and All that is, for the guidance and support that is always with us. The saying "Be still, and know I am" speaks of our connection to God and how to access this connection.

The "Big Bang" is all the expressed and defined information generated from the creative force (God) expanding to its furthest point from the creative force (God), and rebounding in on itself, creating a vibrational reaction and causing the next "Big Bang" with the newly defined creative expressions of conscious energy. Blending all that positively charged outgoing thought with the grounding receptive energy of the visualized fulfillment of the thought realized created a vibrational blending of positively charged outgoing thought with negatively charged receptive feeling, thus producing not a destructive explosion, but its polar opposite – Creation!

Observing how a battery works may help in understanding the dynamics involved. When you combine positively charged outgoing energy with negatively charged receptive energy, the reaction creates a cyclic flow of energy that can be utilized for practical purposes. God has been expressing and evolving these abilities for a really long time, long before time and space were conceived and brought forth into expression. Bottom line: everything that we see as reality in this finite world, our physical bodies included, are expressions of conscious energy that allows us, children of God, to express, define and refine our conscious understanding of who we truly are – pure consciousness.

10

E G O

The evolution of all living things has one purpose: to allow God to define God and God's qualities and to refine those qualities to their highest expression. That which is, is defined in a subjective state of consciousness and brought forth into physical manifestation (objective state), where it can be refined in this relative state of expression. It is this relative awareness that allows God to define God in the most efficient way. The Beast was created to give God a means to express God's selfless impersonal energy as self-centered personal energy, its polar opposite, and then to refine that energy by mixing the personal energy with God's impersonal awareness of all that is, creating God's only begotten son/daughter, the Christ, the perfect blending of the self and the selfless. Ego, which is your sense of self, and the conscious structure that defines each of our unique identities, is the polar opposite of the impersonal structure that creation rides upon, allowing for the relative dynamics necessary to energize our personal lives.

As we exercise aspects of our self-centered identity (Ego - the Beast) that don't serve us, we begin to regain access to the impersonal, selfless awareness that we had prior to the Fall from Innocence. The impersonal awareness of all that is (God) becomes available to us and we once again begin to see the big picture through the eyes of God's selfless awareness.

Now the selfless, impersonal, innocent awareness that was us prior to the Fall becomes infused with a personal awareness of self that allows us to understand, for one thing, Love. Love is very personal, and it is ego and the self-centered side of consciousness that defines love. The selfless, impersonal side of creation does not express love as we know it. Love is personal, and the structure that supports creation is impersonal. It is relative dynamics that link these two polar opposites. It is our self-centered awareness that allows us to understand, feel, and express love. Think about it!

11

THE CHRIST AND THE ANTI-CHRIST

Man is created in our (God's) image. If you believe this statement to be true, then it should cause you to question who exactly are you and what your relationship to God is. First of all, you are God. God and you are one and God is greater. If God is no thing and we are physical beings, how can we be created in God's image? In the Bible, man is created twice. This has confused many people. God, being no thing (pure consciousness), created us first as pure consciousness in God's image.

When we were first born (created), like a little baby, we were in a state of innocence, knowing ourselves only as being one with God. We were yet to have an identity of self (I am), knowing only God's selfless love and ourselves as one with God. God, being All-knowing and wise beyond description, knew we needed to be educated in order to gain a sense of identity greater than that possessed in our innocent, childlike state. This three-dimensional objective realm was created as a means for us to grow into the greatness as children of God that we are and more. It is important to remember that we are eternal beings clothed in physical bodies.

Before we were born we were pure consciousness, and when we die we leave our physical bodies and return to a state of pure consciousness. As physical beings living in this physical realm, we are still pure consciousness. Being in our physical bodies allows us to gain a sense of separation, making it possible to gain a sense of identity that is unique to each and every one of us. What many of us are waking up to is the realization that we are greater than what is contained within our bodies. What we truly are is God (pure consciousness), selfless in nature. All that is, comes from the thoughts and feelings of God. What moves God forward on God's journey of evolution is God's highest vibrational energy. This energy is what we call the Christ.

The Christ is selfless love and the anti-Christ is love of self, which are polar opposites of one another. It is the relative dynamics created by the interaction of self-centered defined desire for creation and the selfless creative force that power the process of creation.

Energy intermixing, pushing back and forth on itself until the energies find a vibrational unity, causes the energy to shift from pushing against itself to pushing together for a unified purpose. The Yin and Yang sign symbolizes this energy. The alignment of opposing forces allows for forward progress, transforming two opposite halves to one empowered whole. This realignment, from repulsion to mutual attraction, emerges from the source of the energy (God/you) observing the interaction of the energy and its effects on its environment.

By observing the thoughts and feelings that support the physical reality in the moment, God (we) can better understand the nature of God's, and our, consciousness. The interaction of thoughts and feelings gives information about the vibrational level of the consciousness that supports the physical expression. What always lies beneath and supports the finite physical expression, be it thought, feeling, or action, is the energy expressing it. How this energy feels is an indicator of the level of the energy being expressed in the moment that it is being expressed. Constructive energy resonates at a higher, more pleasant vibrational level, while destructive energy resonates at a lower, unpleasant level. Your higher selfless energy moves you closer to oneness with your omnipotent, omnipresent supportive energy (God) while your lower self-centered energy creates separation from that energy. Unbalanced, discordant energy causes vibrations within the consciousness that feel unpleasant and heavy. Balanced, positive energy causes vibrations within the consciousness that feel pleasant and uplifting. Thoughts are outgoing energy being expressed. Feelings and intuition come from incoming energy vibrating within our inner consciousness, creating the sensation we know as emotions. Our thoughts are always outgoing and expressive, and our emotions are always incoming and receptive.

Remember, everything comes from the mind of God, brought forth by the intermixing of thought (positive, outgoing energy) and feeling (grounding, receptive energy). It is by separation of the qualities of masculine (+) and feminine (-) energy that creates the elements necessary to power God's creativity.

The blending of these polar opposites brings forth everything that is, from pure consciousness to the densest of physical material. The exercising of the different aspects of any given focus of consciousness precipitates the highest expression of that focus. Simply observing one's thoughts and feelings reveals the truth about what one is conscious of and the energy that is being brought forth. While focusing on what feels correct and letting go of thoughts that create discordant vibrations in one's feeling body, the consciousness grows stronger with the thoughts that prevent one's energy from its highest expression falling away, leaving a clearer, stronger consciousness. Simply moving our attention from the physical event and paying attention to how the energy being expressed creating the physical event feels, gives us a deeper understanding of the energy we send and receive. This is God's version of evolution.

Remember that All that is, is an expression of pure consciousness. Everything that is brought forth into manifestation serves the purpose of expressing consciousness. What is gained is understanding, expanding God's awareness of God and God's ability as a Creator. To bring forth the Christ is to raise the energy of consciousness to its highest level of expression. The Christ is pure selfless energy unencumbered by selfish distractions. The Christ is the perfect blending of God's selfless awareness with pure uncluttered, self-centered focus. The Christ and the anti-Christ have access to both selfless and self-centered conscious energy. What differentiates the Christ from the anti-Christ is that a Christ-like being has invested time and energy in clarifying his or her conscious connection to the greater part of who we are (God) and has clear access to both his or her self-center and God's omnipresent, omnipotent energy, and the wisdom that comes with that connection. The anti-Christ has invested all its energy into self-gratification and has not developed a clear pathway to the greater conscious energy of the creative force, God. The Christ sees everything as it is and understands the connectivity of All that is, making it possible to function at the highest level of strength and understanding. The Christ is God's consciousness raised to its highest level of expression. We come from that consciousness, we *are* that consciousness.

What separates us from God's perfect selfless energy is the anti-Christ. The anti-Christ is self-centered. How can one see all the greatness of All that is if the focus is on the self? You can't see the Heavens looking through a microscope – think about it.

We are eternal beings. To think that our fate lies in the short time we have in just one life is foolish. Our ability to come into physical manifestation, choosing a specific genetic bloodline, and its alignment to God's creative matrix via the time and place of birth that suits our needs for understanding at a given point in our evolution, allows for continual growth. We have lived many lives and will live as many more as we choose on our eternal quest for growth and understanding of our potential as children of God.

Reincarnation was taken out of Christianity by an establishment that wanted to control their subjects with fear. People were told that if they didn't obey the rules set forth by the establishment, they would go to Hell forever; a pretty effective way to control ignorant people. But simple logic makes self-evident the foolishness of this small-minded view of who we truly are. Reincarnation is a very efficient method of gaining knowledge on a multitude of conscious levels reincarnating in and out of this physical finite realm, with each life allowing for the expression of uniquely defined creative abilities to be refined with each life. This is creative evolution in motion.

The countless lives we have lived have allowed us to gain a sense of self. What appears to be separation has been created to allow us to gain our identity. Now that we have a defined sense of self, it's time to begin the challenging process of eliminating aspects of self-centeredness that don't serve our highest expression of self. As we begin to monitor our thoughts and how we feel about our thoughts, our inward attention causes the flow of consciousness to shift to a higher vibrational frequency, which in turn attracts higher vibrational energy and the physical manifestations that it supports.

The energy of the Christ is uplifting, bringing with it feelings of love, gratitude, and joy. The energy of the anti-Christ is heavy, bringing feelings of sadness, anger, and pain. The Christ opens up; the anti-Christ closes down. The Christ sees the big picture; the anti-Christ can't see beyond its self-centered needs. The Christ has infinite patience; the anti-Christ is irresolutely impatient. The anti-Christ is self-centered and functions from its limited self-centered understanding; the Christ understands the connectedness of All that is and acts to bring the energy of the moment to its highest expression for all concerned. The Christ is God's consciousness exercised and raised up to its highest expression. The Christ is perfection refined to its purest state of being. The Christ is All there truly is. It is All that is left once consciousness is raised and refined to its purest state of expression.

From the beginning, God has grown by viewing the state of consciousness that God is experiencing and dwelling on the qualities of that state. The aspects of that state of consciousness that vibrate at the highest level are separated from those that vibrate at the lowest level. This separation of qualities allows for the examination of the state of consciousness, giving defined points of reference. Light, in all its brilliance, can be understood for what it is because of dark. We understand and appreciate good behavior because we have bad behavior to help define it. Everything gets defined in this relative manner.

As the highest and lowest vibrational energies find their natural frequency, it becomes apparent to the observer (us and God) which aspects of consciousness serve growth and which aspects don't. Just like a meal, we take it All in. The beneficial aspects nourish growth and the aspects that do not nourish are eliminated. Yes, the anti-Christ is essentially the big pile of poop that is left once God's greatness has been raised to its highest expression. Turning one's thoughts away from the negative energy of the anti-Christ causes that energy to wither and die. Once it dies, it can be tilled into the soil of one's consciousness, where the wisdom that comes from the experience of raising up one's understanding fuels the next step towards perfection.

The statement "The Christ is God's only begotten son" is a statement of truth. But what does it really mean? Just like a son or daughter bringing forth the energy of his or her parents from one generation to the next, building on the foundation created by his or her parents, the Christ rests upon All that is, God. All the knowledge and wisdom that comes from the knowledge that God has gained from all the experience that God has had from countless Adventures consciously creating are available to us through the Christ. As we let go of the self-centered thoughts and actions that these thoughts support, our consciousness begins to redirect itself from seeing small to understanding the big picture. This simple shift of energy opens up our consciousness to All the selfless energy that animates All that is.

This reunion with All that is (God) brings with it a joy greater than words can describe. It opens up All of God's power and wisdom that animates that power. We begin to gain a connection with everything and everyone. This connection allows us to understand the energy in each and every moment, making it possible to rise up and align our consciousness with God's. The Christ which lies within all of us begins to shine forth into our lives, illuminating each and every moment, raising the energy as we interact with those around us in our everyday lives. When we allow our Christ consciousness to shine forth, it affects everyone we interact with, elevating not only our consciousness but the consciousness of those we interact with. The Christ is immensely powerful, affecting everything it touches. It melts away negativity and raises the vibrational energy, healing, enlightening, and lighting first the one who generates it before rippling out to embrace all those who are open to its positive influence.

God is the most loving, caring, wisest, and most powerful Creator there is, and we are created in God's exact image. Everything that is God's is ours for the asking. All we need to do is go within and ask. If you have children, you understand the love you feel for them. There is nothing you wouldn't do to make their lives more joyous, more meaningful. God has had time before time, ad infinitum, to express love, define love, and refine love to its highest, most perfect expression. This love is pointed straight at you. Do you feel it? It envelops you. There is no place that you can go where God's love is not. You can hide your head and heart in sadness, frustration, anger, hatred, or any state of being that lowers your vibrational energy, but God is always right here, within you and around you. All you need to do is ask. Ask for the Christ to be manifest in your life, to influence your dealings with others, to bring your energy to its highest, most loving level possible.

Pay attention to your thoughts and how those thoughts make you feel. Monitoring your feelings and the thoughts they create sets in motion a process that transforms self-centered energy into a greater, lighter energy that you can elevate to the highest vibrational realm, where true wisdom and power abide. To be born again is to let go of your selfish, self-centered perspective on how your world should be and allow yourself to become reopened to All that is, God!

Understand that we came from a state of oneness with God, knowing ourselves only as God. In this state of innocence, we had no point of reference to allow us to see ourselves apart from God. The fruit that Adam and Eve received from the tree of life was not stolen against God's Will. How could anything be stolen from an omnipotent, omnipresent God that not only sees everything but is everything? This was the gift that has enabled us to discover who we are and what our potential truly is. Remember, we are God, and God is greater. Our connection to God is on the level of consciousness. We will never find God in this physical realm until we find God within ourselves, within our consciousness.

Dying on the cross was the easy part. By the time Jesus made his final walk to the crucifixion, he knew that he was a conscious being clothed in his physical body. He understood his connection to God and knew that his body was the vehicle that allowed him, a conscious child of God, to experience all the opportunities for growth that this physical realm offers. Stepping out of his body was as easy as stepping out of a car once he had reached his destination because Jesus knew who he was, a child of God, pure consciousness clothed in a physical body.

The pain Jesus felt was in his body, not within his consciousness. His understanding made it possible for Jesus to know the difference between the physical pain (what the physical body was feeling) and the pain felt within the depths of the soul. Pain becomes unbearable when we cling to the self-centered, superficial aspects of our lives instead of redirecting our focus outside of our self-centered viewpoint. What we focus on grows and becomes stronger and more defined. Focus on pain and you get pain. Focus on the energy creating pain, viewing the pain as the expression of that energy, and our attention moves from the pain to the positive uplifting loving energy that lies just beyond the pain.

Jesus was not a wimp. He carried the weight of the world on his shoulders. He spent his life conscious of the energy that he carried within himself and was ever-vigilant, constantly monitoring his thoughts and feelings and letting go of the thoughts and feelings that didn't serve his highest expression of self. Getting rid of all negative thoughts and feelings allowed Jesus to receive God's energy without it being diluted or misdirected by ego. The mental and emotional pain that we feel is God's selfless consciousness being blocked by ego (how we see ourselves and our world). By examining our thoughts and feelings, we can let go of that which does not serve our highest expression of self and allow God's selfless brilliance to illuminate our being, giving us access to our spiritual body and All that is, God. Remember, we and God are one and God is greater.

Therefore, the gift that Jesus gave us was not his death. The gift Jesus gave us was his life. He devoted himself to eliminating all aspects of self that did not serve his highest expression of self. He gave of himself and God, using all the love and the light that he gained perfecting himself. All that Jesus did and all that he gained from God did not die; it is right here within each and every one of us, lighting our way to perfection. We can call upon this light at all times. It is omnipresent and omnipotent. It is the Christ and it is God's gift to us, God's children.

Jesus perfecting himself showed us that it can be done. But, more importantly, his efforts cleared away a great deal of negative ego-based energy. Gaining access to the loving energy of the Christ was made easier because Jesus transmuted a great deal of negative ego-based energy, blocking all of our access to the Christ. When Jesus stated that we are all brothers and sisters and what affects the least of us, affects all of us, he spoke of our true identity, pure consciousness clothed in physical bodies. As we become aware of the energy that supports negativity, we begin to see that the physical manifestation of our energy and the consciousness that supports the manifestation are not separate. We can shift our focus from this physical realm of symptoms to the conscious reality where All that is, is created and maintained. We stop pushing on the physical manifestation that our thoughts create and shift our attention to our conscious thoughts and feelings that create and support our physical reality.

If we act with the intention of bringing forth the highest expression that circumstances allow, we become open to every possible course of action. Letting go of our self-centered agenda lightens our load, allows our energy to become more focused, giving us true authentic power to use in our interactions, and imbues us with a feeling of joy that permeates our physical, mental, and spiritual body before spilling out to affect everyone we interact with. Letting go of our ego and allowing ourselves to open up to God's All-knowing wisdom frees up a lot of the energy that we invest in attempting to control our environment. Letting go of our ego entails moving our focus beyond what we want, and balancing our needs with what course of action, thinking, or behavior will best serve the circumstances of each moment of our lives. Simply put, be mindful of yourself and what your interactions with others, and the world in general, create. Be positive and uplifting with others and give more than you take. Balancing our love of self with our selfless love is our purpose for being here and what gives us our creative abilities.

The Fall was our stepping out of the innocence of a child, being loved and cared for by loving parents and emerging into the world of relative dynamics, learning all that God knows and becoming partners with God in God's eternal journey of realization. We are taking the next step on God's eternal family tree. We are supported by All that God is, All that God knows, and All that God desires for God, and us, for we are God. We cannot fail. It is God's will that we succeed, and God always gets what God desires. We are going to grow back into God's loving, all-knowing consciousness. In truth, we never lost our connection to God. It is impossible to become disconnected from God or God's love for us, God's beloved children.

Ask yourself, what do you desire most? What is that desire that is burning deep within your very being? What is it asking you to do? Is it God calling you home? Is it God's loving light patiently waiting for you to turn from your self-centered agenda and face back into the light? When you're ready, God's all-knowing omnipotent, omnipresent consciousness will lift you up out of the limitations your own ego imposes on you and bring you back into the light of conscious living, where you become a co-creator with God, standing in the light with God.

Once we find our connection to God in our highest vibrational energy (love, gratitude, and joy) and begin focusing our thoughts and feelings on this higher energy and the connection to God that it brings, two things happen. First, the incredible feelings of peace and joy that our positive thoughts and feelings produce become infectious. When we feel joyous thoughts, we begin to focus more on the energy of those thoughts and feelings. As we focus on our higher consciousness, our higher, more positive energy becomes more defined and negative energy falls away. Remember that what we focus on grows stronger and what we turn our attention away from will wither and die.

Second, as we become aware of the way that the negative aspects of our ego get in the way and separate us from our connection with God, we begin to shift our energy from trying to control our world to monitoring our thoughts and feelings for the highest expression to bring into our world. This is working in partnership with God and All that is.

An ego-based life is self-centered, requiring that everything goes through and gets approved by the boss, our ego, which means that we must plot our course, push the wagon, and steer along that course. There's not much time to take in the scenery on our journey. A life that is lived consciously connected to God via our highest, most joyous thoughts and feelings frees us to take in all the scenery and appreciate the exquisite beauty of the journey.

A life lived consciously connected to God means expressing our desire to God via our thoughts and feelings. Compare it to programming your desired destination into a navigating computer. This computer knows every possible route, from the largest freeway to the smallest foot path. It knows all the shortcuts and where all the dead ends and cliffs are. Similarly, all we have to do is program our inner computer using our thoughts and feelings. Once your desires have been input, wait for directions from your inner computer (consciousness). Directions come back to you the same way your desires are input to God, through your thoughts and feelings. God's directions always represent the ideal path. The simple shift from trying to control your world to monitoring your thoughts and feelings as you navigate your life creates a selfless flow of energy and a more productive and graceful you.

Conversely, trying to control your world requires self-centered energy. Your focus becomes fixated on your self-centered agenda, unable to see beyond what you are focused on. The process of monitoring and balancing your thoughts and feelings requires that you focus on them and the environment and interactions that you are involved in, in that moment. This simple act causes your attention to open up to what's in the moment. True, authentic power is always available right here, right now in the moment. Our egos tend to take us out of the moment and away from our conscious connection to God and all the true authentic power that is always right here, right now, in this moment.

Understand that space allows us to separate that which our consciousness creates and time allows us to experience the interaction of our thoughts as we bring them forth to intermingle with the conscious energy of others in an orderly manner. While time and space allow us to separate conscious thoughts and experience and the effects of those thoughts in a defined, timely manner, we are meant to live in the moment where our connection to All that is (God) always exists. It is dwelling on the pain of the past and the anxiety for the future that keeps us out of the moment where our true power and our true connection to God is. Everything that has ever happened, happened in the moment.

God is always right here, right now in this moment – always has been and always will be. Our connection to God lies within our thoughts and feelings in this moment. God dwells in Heaven, and Heaven is up, up in the highest vibratory realm of thought and feeling. In order for us to abide in a conscious state of oneness with God, we must progress beyond being tightly contained, self-centered, self-focused beings. Living in the moment allows us to monitor and balance our thoughts and feelings and learn to let go of those that don't serve our highest expression of self.

This is what Jesus did to become the embodiment of the Christ. Was it God's Will? Yes. Was everything necessary for Jesus to fulfill God's Will always right there right now to support Jesus? Yes. But Jesus had to exercise aspects of self-centeredness that did not vibrate in the highest conscious realm of Heaven. Jesus allowed his focus to turn away from self and be redirected to always see the big picture in every moment. What Jesus did, we are meant to do, and greater.

Knowing that Heaven is the realm of consciousness, Jesus lived consciously, seeing the physical as symptoms of consciousness and healed people by consciously raising the vibration of the conscious energy of the person he was healing. Jesus knew that the physical realm is supported by the conscious realm and by consciously raising the energy of the person in the body, the body has to heal. That's the gift Jesus was born with, a transcendent greatness that God bestowed upon him. Though it came wrapped in poop – his ego – his efforts to balance himself and clear away aspects of self that didn't serve his highest, most loving expression allowed him to transcend the limitations of ego. Yes, God gave him everything and yes, he became worthy of the Gift.

Jesus said, "The things I do, you will do, and greater." Jesus laid the foundation for us to stand on. His life showed what to do to become the embodiment of the Christ. But what incredible Gift of greatness lies within you, wrapped in the poop of your self-centeredness, waiting to shine forth? Letting go of your self-centered focus and bringing your focus into the moment right here, right now, is all that is necessary to begin your personal remembering and rebirth into your conscious oneness with God, All that is. The key is simply letting go and letting God.

Many of us are ready to leave our childish ways and step into the light of the Christ, willing to live God's big, selfless plan for growth into more and more understanding of God's (our) limitless abilities. The Christ, God's selfless love, is our path back to conscious oneness with God (walking with God). The Christ is selfless, operates at the highest vibrational realms of consciousness, and can only be accessed through positive, loving, selfless thoughts and feelings.

12

W H O ' S   D R I V I N G

We are eternal beings and we are perfect. But if this is true, then how do we explain all the imperfection in the world? How do we explain death? Blame it on the vehicle. That thing that you see in the mirror when you're brushing your teeth is finite and you, the person within is infinite. The eternal being within is an aspect of God, the person you call you is the vehicle that is allowing you to express, define, and refine your conscious energy. The person whom you chose to be in this life has qualities that were defined at the moment of your conception. There is a balance of strengths and weaknesses that came with who you are. This balance of energy is not who you, the eternal being, is, but an expression of the energy that you are working with on your eternal quest to know yourself as God. Having the infinite wisdom that we possessed prior to our birth, and the understanding that came with that wisdom, we chose to be who we are knowing that the vehicle that is who we now are makes available all the necessary ingredients required for growth as an eternal spiritual being.

What you learn on this Adventure is supported by the specific energy that brought you into this world at the time of your birth. The energy that is you is unique to you and this energy allows you to express your conscious awareness in your own unique manner. You receive energy filtered through the conscious matrix that you came into this life with and express energy back out through this same filter.

The trick is to stay in the moment and focus your conscious energy inward, paying attention to its vibrational resonance as you entertain the thoughts and feelings that arise. We spend much of our conscious energy outside of ourselves on the events of our lives that tend to distract us from our inner connection with All that is, God. Focusing outside of ourselves puts control into the hands of the vehicle, weakening the eternal being's influence on the events that occur.

The person you see in the mirror is the self-centered side of the equation; the person within is the selfless side of the conscious being that you are. The self-centered side allows you to get into the Adventure, much like standing in the forest and interacting with the trees and all that the Adventure allows. The problem is that from this perspective, you can't see the forest from the trees. The trick is to still your thoughts (stop generating outgoing conscious energy) and receive the conscious sustenance that is always available. You can't talk and listen at the same time. If you are always sending conscious energy, you aren't open to receive much of God's conscious support.

God is not separate from you; never has been and never will be. When you feel alone and separated from God, it's because you're sending, not receiving, conscious energy. The saying "be still and know I am" is all about learning to quiet your thoughts and feelings in order to receive God's conscious nourishment. God doesn't hear whimpering and whining. The energy that comes from negative thoughts and feelings doesn't make it to Heaven, where God abides. The vibrational energy is too low. That is why we don't ask for things we want. Wanting is a confirmation of lack and is therefore of a lower vibrational energy.

We are told to thank God for that which we desire because gratitude and the joy of fulfillment is of the highest vibrational energy and has the means to attract all the necessary ingredients for the fulfillment of our desires. Remember, light (consciousness) was the first ingredient that brought forth our reality at the time of the "Big Bang," and as children of God, we have the very same creative skills. We just have to remember who we are and in whose image we were created. If we, the eternal beings who dwell within the flesh, choose to invest our conscious energy by stilling our thoughts and feelings so we can hear God's guidance, which is always right here, right now in the moment, our lives will become more meaningful and our Adventure will become more graceful, creative, and joyous.

13

T H E   G I F T

We come from a state of conscious oneness with All that is, God. The facts support this truth. We now live in a state of physical separation, with everything being defined not by its commonalities but by its unique individual characteristics. These two facts seem to be in conflict with one another at first glance, but deeper examination reveals the truth about their interrelationship. Where we get confused is in the self-centered side of the equation. We have forgotten the part about us being eternal conscious beings, consciously connected to All that is (God). This is the We aspect of our identity. This We aspect of our identity has been undergoing a process of definition from the very beginning and is the foundation on which everything stands. Our I am, the exact opposite of the eternal We, is what We are here to express, define, and refine. This process is what allows God to be omnipotent and omnipresent, seeing everything with the accuracy that comes from a personal perspective, balanced with the conscious understanding of the big picture. Understand that your ego filters information en route to your I am (your sense of who you are), obscuring truth and making it impossible to see the big picture.

Remember that we are conscious eternal beings, consciously connected to All that is. We are literally God, and God is greater. What does this mean? Where we tend to get lost is in our sense of self, who we think we are in order to have the adventures necessary for us to gain our I am (our identity). It is necessary that we approach the Adventure with the feeling that is reality, allowing us to invest ourselves in the process of building our individual sense of self. If we understand who we truly are, we would not make the choices we tend to make due to our limited understanding and would not create as much poop in our lives. However, it's poop that makes things grow and we are here to grow. It is the process of looking at the events of our lives and how our actions serve our best interests that causes us to grow consciously.

We must realize that what others do to us is far less important than what we do with what others do to us. As we grow, we come to realize that it is our understanding that is eternal, not the shiny trinkets that are the source of so much distraction from what matters. We bring conscious awareness with us when we are born, and we build on that conscious foundation using the tools we have learned from past experiences.

Life is like a feast. The hunger within our souls is very much like physical hunger. We decide what to experience from the menu that our lives bring us. Like a meal, our experiences have aspects that nourish us and cause us to grow, and aspects that don't. If we live consciously aware lives, we are able to process the information life's experiences bring us, allowing for conscious evolution, away from the Me side of consciousness and back towards the We side of who we truly are, and with All that is, God. We will never lose our I am, but rather clarify it, allowing us to become anchored in All that is, God.

When completed, this process brings us to the point that Jesus spoke of: to stand equal with God, and to have access to all of God's omnipotent, omnipresent power. We are not the first nor will we be the last to go through this Adventure. This is how God expands consciously. God has learned from countless experience, stretching well beyond time and space, the most effective way to get what God wants: understanding. The very first tick of conscious energy that gave God God's "I am" made self-evident a great deal of information. And, at that moment, God knew all that God had witnessed. God's ability to take all that God knows and manipulate the conscious energy of that knowing allows for new expressions of that knowledge to become self-evident, causing the evolution of understanding. God wants to know everything, and the more God knows, the more it becomes apparent what can be learned. While it is true that God knows everything that is known, there will always be more to learn, and that is what drives God. Look at what drives us and you will realize that we are created in God's conscious image, and our connection lies within. That is the Gift of our oneness with God (all that is). Can you think of a more precious Gift?

14

BORN AGAIN

Being born again – what does that mean? We come from a state of oneness with All that is, God. In this state of consciousness, we knew ourselves as God, and were yet to acquire our sense of self, or I am. With the Fall, our focus was shifted from the We side of who we are (God) and reoriented, allowing us to define a unique identity and giving each of us our own sense of self.

As we gain experience and the wisdom necessary to utilize all of God's conscious energy, we begin to fill our minds with information. As we learn the truth about our experience (the nourishing part of the meal), we gain wisdom that allows us to express and define conscious energy in our own specific way. As we gain wisdom about what is the truth, we also take in information that runs contrary to the truth. For example, as we learn to get our own way, we become more self-focused, which creates a stronger sense of self (I am) but also pulls our attention away from our connection to God, creating a conscious separation that makes us stronger or weaker, depending on whether we clarify our conscious connection with inward introspection or choose to focus only on getting our own way.

This conscious separation of the We side of consciousness from the Me side of self is like lengthening your conscious lever. If we focus our attention on what's going on outside of ourselves, without balancing our conscious energy by going within and asking the question "How does this serve me?", we become more separated from our connection with All that is, God. Investing the time and effort to go within and observe what's going on consciously with our thoughts and feelings will allow us to eliminate the conscious clutter we acquire in our daily lives, giving us a strong connection between the Me part of who we are, and the We (God) side of who we are providing us with more conscious leverage.

As we grow older and expand our conscious awareness, we can strengthen our connection between the Me side of who we are becoming and the We side of who we truly are. This effort will keep us childlike, in the sense of being open to truth, but with the strength and grace that comes with a strong conscious connection to God, and All that is.

Jesus was consciously reborn by using this process. This is what is known as the virginal birth, shedding all the aspects of ego that veiled our connection with God. Jesus' forty days in the desert were not spent wrestling with a devil but with his own ego. It's like the familiar cartoon trope where a character is struggling with a dilemma and has the devil perched on one shoulder and an angel on the other, each giving opposing advice. The devil argues for selfish gratification while the angel explains the benefits of the big picture.

Jesus spent his entire life balancing his conscious energy. Jesus spent a fair amount of his time alone with himself communing with God. He did so in order to still his mind from the distractions of his world and balance the thoughts within his conscious being. His forty days in the desert represent the culmination of his efforts to move consciously into the realm of loving light that supports All that is on the highest vibrational levels of creation. This is the realm where we can tap into God's loving energy and utilize it to heal and manifest on the highest level.

All that God has is truly ours; we just have to know how to gain access. God can always be accessed. Our connection can't be broken, and it's at the highest vibrational rate of love and light that we gain access to God's realm as Creators, born again and living consciously connected to Heaven while here on earth.

15

ANGELS

Do you believe in Angels? Angels are seen as beings of light, not physical, but yet human in appearance. They appear humanlike because they are tasked with the very personal privilege of interacting with us humans, up close and personal, assisting us on a higher conscious level. They are able to get as spiritually close and personal as we (our egos) will allow them to. Their vibrational conscious energy is just above ours, and when we raise our hearts and minds up in love and gratitude, we link into their energy, which amplifies our own conscious energy, allowing us to anchor ourselves deeper in God's omnipotent, omnipresent energy. We are connected to All that is (God) through a conscious grid (matrix) that links each of us; God at God's most personal expression, to God at God's most impersonal (the mechanism that animates creation) supportive energy. Our Angels are our closest most personal connection to all of God's energy.

Do you understand the dynamics involved in this ongoing Adventure? We receive an incredible amount of conscious support from the omnipotent, omnipresent infinite realm of creation (Heaven). We simply must be still, and go within, to be aware of its presence. We tend to forget that our connection to God and All that is is a conscious connection and we look outside ourselves for a God that is separate from us. We forget that we and God are one and God is greater. It is impossible for God not to be right here, right now all the time. We just need to turn our attention inward, be still, and listen for the guidance that is always available. We are always being touched, protected, and guided by God. What we see as Angels are, just like us, aspects of All that is, God.

Understand that you are God at God's most personal expression. You will never get any closer to God than you are right now because

49

you *are* God. What will change is your awareness of who and what you truly are. That is why we are here; to gain understanding, expanding our conscious awareness away from our innocent perspective, defining who we are, and by going within, refining our conscious pathway to the greater part of who we truly are, God. We never lose our closeness to God, we just accumulate conscious clutter that veils our connection. But by going within and clarifying our conscious clutter, we maintain our closeness to God's omnipresent energy. This is how God has become omnipotent and omnipresent. Each of us represents a point of focus of God's omnipotent, omnipresent awareness of All that is, God. As we expand our self-awareness, we increase God's omnipotent, omnipresent energy. That is what this Adventure is all about: growth, both ours and God's.

You are God at God's most personal expression. You are God being self-centered. Think of yourself as the bull's eye of a target. What would be as far from the self-centered perspective that is you is the selfless and impersonal structure that supports our lives, and creation. This is the aspect that moves the planets and binds the cosmos. This aspect of God controls the inner workings of creation on a grand scale but is not focused on the details that unfold from creation's expressed energy. This selfless aspect of God does not bend to our self-centered needs. It is we who must learn to adjust to God's plan that was set forth at the time of the "Big Bang."

So, if you are God at God's most personal expression, and the cosmos and creation are riding on the most impersonal aspect of God consciousness, the question becomes, what bridges the impersonal (God) to the personal (you)? What we think of as Angels link God, the impersonal, with us; God at God's most personal expression. The bull's eye represents us, and the outermost ring represents God at the most impersonal level where the cosmos, our bodies included, are bound, sustained, and animated. The concentric rings that bridge the selfless aspect of God to you, the bull's eye, are what we see as Angels. We are always being touched by God, we are God, and God is greater.

You have Angels that are here to watch over and assist you. That is their job 24/7. They will not impose God's Will upon you but are here to help you bridge your conscious energy to the greater conscious energy of All that is, God. If you choose to express low or discordant energy, your Angels will honor your choice. However, if you choose to elevate your conscious energy, they will be excited to assist you. You are the greatest gift that God has blessed them with.

The ability to interact with us and assist us in creating our reality enables our Angels to expand their conscious awareness, growing closer to their own eternal potential. Just like us, Angels are here to express, define, and refine conscious energy. While they are not here in physical form experiencing the heaviness of this finite realm, they are still here balancing energy. Much of their work is in assisting us in balancing the energy that life's lessons bring us. The joy we bring to our Angels and God when we are in tune with our higher conscious energy resonates throughout creation, affecting ourselves, those people we interact with, our Angels themselves, and God at the very heights of Heaven. When we function at our higher vibrational range of consciousness, our energy becomes linked to the higher creative side of our reality, allowing us to co-create our lives as they unfold. This is far more evolutionary than living with our energy down in the lower, fear-based realm of creation, where we are left to react to the ebb and flow of reality as it unfolds, one or two steps behind as we constantly struggle to regain balance.

Taking the time to go within and know yourself gives you access to the greater wisdom of your Angels and of creation, empowering your life. As we become aware of the creative side of our reality and of our conscious connection to our Angels and their limitless support, we realize that our connection to God is truly omnipotent and omnipresent and runs from the very personal (you), supported by your personal Angels, all the way to the grandest, most impersonal conscious energy that supports, sustains, and animates this Adventure we see as reality.

What bridges you, your Angels, and the impersonal mechanics of creation is a multitude of varied conscious energy. This energy causes your conscious feelings to ebb and flow, and supports your personal conscious energy, binds the molecules in your body, and animates the cosmos along with many other things filling in the void between the personal (you) and the impersonal. You're the bull's eye. The first ring represents your personal Angel, the second ring represents the Angels that watch over your family group, the third ring represents the Angels that watch over your community group, the fourth ring represents your national group and so on, all the way to the most impersonal mechanism of creation. Can you sense the overlap of conscious energy bathing us and everything in its supportive light? Nothing gets overlooked or is left without support. The abundance of energy, distributed along various conscious levels, affects everything. You are being touched by God along many facets. Words cannot express the incredible energy that supports you, the infinite child of God, and your finite body on this Adventure called life. Be still and feel yourself, your Angels, and God.

16

L O V E

Love is warm and fuzzy and everyone relishes the feeling. But where does love come from and what are its dynamics? We overlook the fact that our established reality had to be expressed and defined for us to experience it. So, the question becomes: how did love come to be defined? The answer is relative.

Truth is self-evident, and when God's eternal selfless awareness turned in on itself and God became aware of God, two distinct perspectives were established: selfless awareness and self-awareness. This relative dance that has been going on from the beginning has crafted our present reality. Love has evolved from the personal side of God's I am. You can imagine how excited you'd feel realizing that you are you. Ever wonder why babies smile so much? They're excited to be here. This realization evolved into the love of self, along with the desire to protect this newfound consciousness. As God learned to express conscious energy in a multitude of different defined expressions, the One (God) became many, allowing for exchanges of this personal conscious energy to define the beginnings of what has evolved into love.

In the animal kingdom, true love manifests in different ways among different species. Look at what a lion will do to protect his pride, or the lengths to which a mother will go to sacrifice herself for her offspring. These conscious characteristics we share with the animal kingdom. What makes us greater than the beasts is our God-given ability to elevate our conscious perspective from our self-centered perspective up into the higher conscious realm of understanding the big picture. What makes us greater than the Angels is that the Angels are limited to the more impersonal big picture and lack the self-centered personal experience that has given us the relative understanding of joy and sadness, gratitude and anger, love and hate that make us more conscious (self-aware).

Love is our road home. It raises our energy up into the realm of creation and Heaven. Self-centered love (being in love) is powerful. Selflessly desiring for others can be considerably more powerful because your love is stretching farther from your self-center to the very heights of creation (Heaven), creating a powerful creative circuit to creation itself. This energy, if consciously directed, can be extremely powerful.

Love is a very powerful dynamic, impressive in its depth from self-centered love to the most selfless acts of sacrifice, offering many creative uses if we choose to exercise our ability to express it. It is also our beacon light that will always, without fail, help us to orient ourselves to our highest purpose, Heaven and God. We are always feeling. If we practice keeping our conscious energy up, in the higher realm of joy, gratitude, and love, we benefit physically, mentally, emotionally, and spiritually. Moreover, the people we interact with will love our energy and act reciprocally. Love is the road home, back into the light, the love and the All-enveloping creative power of All that is, God. Love has many frequencies ranging from self-centered to selfless. Love can be self-gratifying, or selflessly bringing gratification to others. Self-centered love encompasses the one expressing it. Selfless love encompasses the one expressing it and all others it is directed at, and is more powerful than self-centered love. The more love encompasses, the more powerful the love becomes.

Your birthright is written in love, and All that God has is already yours. You are perfect! Living a life focused in the higher conscious realm of joy, gratitude and love will melt away the poop that we tend to get on this Adventure, leaving us lighter and more capable of expressing love.

17

HEAVEN

In many of the stories of ancient wisdom, people are taken to Heaven, where they receive teachings and understandings from the Creator (God). Have you ever wondered where you go when your body sleeps? Have you noticed that quite often you wake up after a night's sleep with answers to challenges you have been facing? This is because when we fall asleep, our ego lies down, so to say, and allows our conscious energy to rise to the higher creative frequencies of Heaven where we are bathed in God's sustaining energy and the wisdom that comes with it. Sleep allows our physical bodies to rest. While we rest, we connect with God and Heaven in a state of conscious awareness at a higher level than we can access through our egos while we're awake. It is the act of setting aside our egos that gains us access to Heaven and God's wisdom.

If God is no thing (pure consciousness), then simple logic would dictate that Heaven is no place. When asked where Heaven is, most people point up. Heaven is indeed up, not physically, but vibrationally. Heaven is pure consciousness expressed at its highest, most loving vibrational level. Heaven is light and joyous. You can't be in Heaven without feeling the joy, love, and gratitude that this energy causes when you express yourself at this high level of being. You can go to Heaven at any time and at any place that you are; it doesn't matter what the circumstances are. It doesn't matter if your environment is calm and joyous or hectic and discordant. You don't need any tools except your ability to feel loving, joyous, gratitude.

Like any skill, it takes practice to become proficient. When you wish to elevate your vibrational frequency to Heaven, think loving and joyous thoughts that cause a feeling of gratitude, joy, and love (imagine the most special person in your world has just appeared unexpectedly and is giving you the best hug you have ever experienced). These focused thoughts will raise your feeling body's vibrational frequency to a higher, more pleasant expression instantaneously and amazingly with little effort.

With enough practice, you will become familiar with the energy supporting loving, joyous gratitude, and you can move away from needing to imagine yourself into this state of being, and learn to maintain this vibrational level of being by paying attention to your energy and what causes it to move up and down vibrationally. Lighten up and you can live in a state of Heaven. When life knocks your vibrational level down, know you can raise yourself up with loving, joyous gratitude. This is a very powerful tool. Pay attention and live in the light!

18

C R E A T I O N

Reality as we perceive it is complex and chaotic, with everything from light to lead being expressed in a myriad of ways. What are the dynamics that bring all this stuff into existence?

For creation to occur, there first must be a desire to create. Desire is receptive in nature and is represented in the Book of Genesis as Eve convincing Adam to pick the fruit. Before Eve could ask Adam to pick the fruit, the desire first had to be defined. Eve's conversation with the snake represents the desire to shed the present state of conscious awareness (the state of conscious innocence). In order for a snake to grow, it must shed its skin (its present state) in order to allow for expansion from within. The snake's new state comes from within itself and is expressed as its new outer state. Desire, which can be associated with intuitive receptivity and the grounding side of creation, starts the process of creation. This requires the positive outgoing energy, its polar opposite, to define and create the vibrational energy necessary, igniting the spark that impregnates the receptive half of the creative force with the energy of the wish in its state of completion, bringing forth the matrix (let there be light) that attracts the necessary ingredients for the realization of the desire in its state of completion.

Creation begins with desire, which is intuitive, receptive, and grounding [negative terminal of a battery (-)] in nature. Defining what the desire is becomes an intellectual outgoing positive process [positive terminal of a battery (+)]. Once the form of the desire in its state of completion becomes defined (creation requires a blueprint), the energy is turned back on itself, creating what science labels a "Big Bang." This is not an explosion but rather a vibrational expression of excited positive energy intermingling with receptive grounding energy, causing a reaction that we see as creation.

Understanding the dynamic flow of energy throughout nature is helpful for gaining knowledge of the force that animates this finite realm because its infinite energy cannot be measured, but its effects on finite matter can. The saying "As above, so below" speaks of this effect infinite energy has on this finite realm. Understanding the simple dynamics of creation makes for a more enlightened and productive life, harnessing the natural flow of creation to help you achieve self-realization as a child of God.

19

TRUTH

If God is no thing (pure consciousness) and there is no thing that is not God, and God is omnipotent and omnipresent, then simple logic tells us that God is every thing, us included (we and God are one and God is greater). If God is truth and All there is, then how can there be so many blatant untruths? Think about it. Remember, all there is is God and God's truth.

In God's eternal search for truth, God gains understanding by focusing awareness upon a subject that God wishes to understand more fully. God experiences every angle of the truth: up, down, in, out, what the truth is, and what the truth is not. Knowing what the truth is *not* is very important for understanding what the truth *is*. It is the ability to adjust, twist, and tweak that truth that enables God (us) to see the truth about the truth. Think about it. To truly understand light, you need dark to help define it. How would light look without dark? Would it be bright? We wouldn't know without having some means of comparison. God has always known all that God knew, and the scope and depth of God's understanding has always made self-evident the next apparent truth. If this were not true, there would be no conscious evolution, and God's reality could not exist.

Bending the truth about pure white light is what gave God (us) all the different colors of the rainbow. So the question is, if truth can be tweaked and adjusted to create new truths, at what point and how does the truth become a lie? A real quick way to turn truth into a lie is to adjust the truth to serve self-centered needs. To take a selfless truth and make adjustments to serve a self-centered agenda creates an imbalance in that truth. It may go unnoticed to the untrained eye, but there is an imbalance nonetheless. But at what point does it become a lie? How many self-centered adjustments to a truth can be made before it becomes a lie or something other than the truth? Look at rules or laws that have been amended to serve special interest groups and it is easy to see how a truth that serves many can be turned into a lie that serves a few, at the expense of many.

20

EXERCISING EGO

We gain and strengthen ourselves (our I am) by getting our way in this Adventure called life. Achieving what we desire defines and strengthens our sense of self. Trying and failing in our endeavors inhibits our sense of who we are and creates insecurity, which can also strongly influence who we think we are. The glory of success and the pain of defeat both affect our sense of self and are among the relative possibilities that this Adventure is defined by.

In the Garden of Eden, there is no such thing as failure, or crash and burn, fall on your rump and get bruised, or beat the competition and win the day. All there is in that state of conscious awareness is the truth of what is. Instead of everything being hot or cold, up or down, dark or light, the relative definition of things lacks the separation between what is, and what is not, to define them. What gives us more potential conscious power than the Angels is our "Fall" into self-centered awareness. Our conscious awareness is more self-centered than that of the Angels. The Angels see themselves as God and lack the ability to comprehend a reality that comes from a self-centered perspective. The Angels' understanding comes from their selfless conscious connection to God. Our self-centered perspective permits us to consciously stand back and understand the separation of what is from what it is not.

While the Angels are consciously standing in God's omnipotent, omnipresent awareness, limited to the Creator's side of understanding, our Fall into the self-centered side of consciousness allows us both the perspective of the Creator and the created. The Angels see themselves as one with everything, as being connected to everything, and lack the experience to understand the separation of the forest and the trees. Our self-centered conception of self allows us to stand in the forest and experience each and every tree as its own unique expression. We possess the conscious ability to view reality with the wisdom of the Creator and/or the view of the created, giving us a perspective greater than that of the Angels.

Think of the We side of consciousness (God) as the brains, perceiving everything, understanding everything, and conceiving everything, but lacking the means to bring it into expression. It is the blending of selfless energy with the self-centered energy that creates reality that can be experienced from a personal perspective. Our conscious separation from the We side of consciousness (the Fall) gave us the ability to create, using the We side of our consciousness, and then stand in it and experience the effects of our creation.

Before the Fall spoken of in Genesis, we had the understanding of an architect (a Creator). After the Fall, we are now learning to swing a hammer and understand all the details of constructing that which we have conceived. The Angels understand the blueprint but lack the strength and experience to swing the hammer and actually construct from the blueprint of creation. Learning to swing our creative hammers required that we turn away from the Creator side of who we are and focus on stepping out of the office (Heaven), put down the blueprints, and start banging nails and an occasional thumb.

Understand that the plans are always drawn before construction begins. The architect (God) sees the big picture and understands how the project is meant to turn out. But if you've been involved in construction, you know that issues come up that were not anticipated during the planning stage. Our ability to get down into the construction zone and deal with the chaos that always comes with creation and consult the architect (God) to make adjustments to the project is what makes us greater than the Angels. The trick is remembering the process of clearing the conscious clutter that we accumulate during our daily lives by taking the time to still our minds, and receive the wisdom that lies just beneath the noise of our daily experiences.

We spend much of our time with our attention outside of ourselves, dwelling on the past or being anxious about the future, forgetting that our power is right here, right now. Everything that has ever been created or ever will be created is created right here, right now, in the moment. This is where our power can always be found. We are conscious eternal beings, clothed in physical bodies that allow us to experience creation from a self-centered perspective.

What we see as reality is in truth a finite expression of infinite consciousness and is an illusion because it remains only as long as the conscious energy that supports it is focused on it. Being focused on physical reality means that we are reacting to the flow of events in our lives, one or two steps behind creation. We need to remember that everything is an expression of conscious energy and is here to allow us to experience, express, define, and refine that conscious energy. We exercise our ego and refine our conscious awareness by turning our attention inward, quieting our thoughts and feelings, and observing the flow of conscious energy. A question that we should ask ourselves often is: how does this given action, thought, or feeling serve me? We invest much of our conscious energy on thoughts or activities that don't feel good and deplete our energy, moving us away from our connection to God, and All that is.

Much of our attention and conscious energy are focused on the finite, superficial manifestations of our conscious energy as we express ourselves in our daily lives, without realizing that the conscious energy we put out dictates what manifests in our lives. Much like using a computer, if we pay attention to what we are inputting, what shows up on the screen is constructive and to our liking. However, if we fixate on the screen (our physical lives) without paying attention to what we are inputting with our conscious energy, we end up with something other than what we intended, and have to deal with the mess. By focusing less attention on the physical events of our lives and more on how the events are affecting us consciously, we begin to eliminate conscious clutter that obscures the truth and zaps our energy. It is our conscious awareness that we bring with us, it is our conscious awareness that we use to negotiate life, and it is our refined conscious awareness that we take with us when we leave this physical realm. It is the currency and what is of true value in our lives.

The impersonal and personal aspects of conscious energy give the relative separation necessary to express and support God's and our adventure of expression. We are leaning towards the self-centered side of who we are right now on our journey of self-discovery. The more self-centered we become, the stronger our I am can become. The trick is to take the time to refine the conscious energy that we take in during our daily lives.

Refining our conscious energy is like practicing martial arts. Yes, you can read the book and gain an understanding of the dynamics involved, but you need to practice the techniques. Mastery comes from the dedication of first learning the techniques and then faithfully practicing them until they become refined to the point of perfect expression. Learning to go off by yourself and move your thoughts and feelings from a focus outside yourself and calmly observe the energy that lies just beneath those thoughts and feelings within will, with practice, give you the ability to direct your life from the strength of your conscious energy, which is much more productive than reacting to the finite expressions of others' misdirected, somewhat unconscious energy.

21

THE MOMENT

We live in a fast-paced world dominated by the ceaseless movement of the clock, yet we tend to take time for granted, rarely pausing to stop and observe the dynamics involved. The question is, are we moving through time, or is it time that is moving as we simply stand in the moment, experiencing its effects? Don't overlook how much support we have in our evolution as conscious children of God. One of these helpers is time and space. So, how does it work?

First, understand that everything is an expression of conscious energy whose purpose is to allow God and us to express, define, and refine our self-awareness. Time and space were created to allow for the expression and evolution of understanding. Nevertheless, you are an infinite being, transcending time and space. Understand that we existed before the "Big Bang" initiated time and space, and we will continue to exist once time and space has completed this particular expression of itself, on this cycle of finite conscious expression (our current reality). What we and God receive from the experience is understanding, and greater creative abilities which we take with us from lifetime to lifetime, and "Big Bang" to "Big Bang," supporting our eternal conscious evolution.

The moment of the "Big Bang," everything that would ever get defined in this material realm was expressed as energy, creating the matrix that supports this thing we call reality. When prophets look into the future, they are reading the matrix that supports this physical realm, not a reality yet to be expressed.

In astrology, each planet represents specific energy that has its own unique rhythm and expressed energy. Astrology tends to view each planet's energy separately, but the energy that supports the planets' alignment with each other and their movement through the cosmos exists as a single mechanism. As the energy of the matrix moves, we see its effects in the physical movement of the cosmos. We also feel its effects within ourselves.

If you pay attention, you will notice that your feelings are always changing. This is supported by the movement of the matrix and your unique alignment to it. This energy, and its movement as the alignment changes, assists in the evolution of all that is, us included. This energy is all-encompassing, omnipotent, omnipresent, and we are always immersed in it. It is what binds and supports every element of which we and our reality are composed.

You are God and God is greater! You are God at God's most personal expression and your personal perspective (your I am) is the lens through which time and space are moving. If you pay attention, you will notice that everything that has ever happened to you, every thought, feeling, and action that you have ever experienced, happened in the moment. To many, this concept may be confusing because all the memories they have experienced throughout their lives appear to be strung out over time. It may be helpful to take a sentimental journey through your life's events and stop to notice that each event occurred in the present moment of your life and was filed in chronological order. Consider life as a pearl necklace, with time being the chord that binds the pearls. Each pearl represents a moment in your life, but the only pearl on the necklace you can touch is the one you are presently experiencing. You can't touch yesterday or tomorrow but you always have access to the moment, which is where all creation always occurs. Everything that is to happen to you will also occur in this eternal moment. We are Creators and creation always happens in the moment. Pay attention!

22

K A R M A

Karma is the energy that supports our progress in this three-dimensional physical Adventure. Karma is a relative energy. It is the Great Balancer. Our conscious focus helps us to define; karma helps us to refine that which we define.

The energy we put out by thinking and feeling about something is karmic energy. As we feel about something, those feelings radiate from our feeling body like ripples on a still pond, until they find energy that is of the same vibrational level. If you exude angry energy, the universe will bring to you corresponding energy and the physical manifestation that will allow you to experience all aspects of that energy — good, bad, or indifferent. Until that energy is refined into only that which serves your highest good, you will feel the dis-ease of the unbalanced energy pulling on you.

Karma has one purpose: to refine energy to its highest potential. It does so by matching the energy we exude to available, like energy. If you wish to change the experiences you keep having (and if you pay attention, you will see a pattern), change the way you think and feel about them. As your attitude and feelings change, your perspective will evolve into a higher truth. As your understanding is refined, you again will balance the energy of this newly refined truth, producing a more refined truth, and the finite results of that new truth.

Our purpose for being is to express conscious energy in our own unique manner, producing a myriad of personal perspectives and adding to God's omnipotent omnipresence. As we gain experience and grow consciously, we take in information that gives each of us our unique abilities. With each experience, we acquire energy in the form of thoughts and feelings. Some of this energy resonates with who we are and adds to our strengths, and some of the energy works contrary to our highest expressions of who we are. As we express ourselves interacting with others, our energy intermingles, causing finite reactions from our infinite conscious energy, which can cause friction if the energy is discordant. This creates karmic energy that gets expressed in our daily lives, which enables us to experience the physical effects of our conscious energy as we express it, allowing those paying attention to refine their conscious energy to a higher, more productive level. That is evolution.

Jesus told us to forgive our enemies, knowing that they were a manifestation of our conscious energy (thoughts and feelings) that would continue producing more enemies until the conscious energy was adjusted to a higher, more loving creative energy. Remember, we get to create, and then stand in it. Create wisely.

23

P A I N

What is the purpose of pain? It shows up in our physical bodies, our mental bodies, our emotional bodies, and our spiritual bodies. Pain tells us when something is broken or out of alignment within our body, sending signals through our nervous system to alert us that something is wrong. This discomfort causes us to make adjustments to alleviate the source of the problem. When something is broken or misaligned in the body, it causes the energy within the body to vibrate at a discordant rate of vibration. It is the unbalanced energy that causes us to feel pain. As the energy gets balanced and the vibrational rate of the energy is raised, the physical body heals.

For the body to heal physically, the energy that supports it must be healed. All the countless atoms dancing to and fro within our bodies do so according to the pure consciousness that is who we are. It is this energy that binds all the atoms of our bodies together and tells them what they are and what their function is. Our physical bodies are what they are because this pure consciousness tells them what they are. When this energy gets disrupted, it manifests as pain in the physical body. When we behave in a way that causes pain to our bodies, we need to look at our physical behavior and the energy behind our behavior that is causing the pain.

Remember, this world we live in is a means for us to express ourselves, define who we are, and to refine that expression of self to its highest level. Without pain to inform us when our energy is out of balance, we would act contrary to our best interest. Pain tells us to stop jumping out of second story windows. The first time hurts, the second time hurts even more, and third time, if we are foolish enough, could cause lasting damage.

Pain also tells us when our emotions are out of balance. It tells us that a given feeling is counterproductive or self-inhibiting. It alerts us to the need to make changes in our thought process to bring joy back into our feeling body. The empty pain we feel deep down in the depths of our souls tells us that we have moved away from the energy that supports our journey towards self-realization of our perfect expression of self.

For most people, pain is something to be avoided at all costs. When experiencing pain, we want a pill or some other quick fix to make it go away. We look for the easy way out instead of addressing the true source that is causing it. But seeing pain as a positive thing, as a tool even, can be deeply empowering. Everything has a purpose. Once we come to this understanding, our lives take on a new meaning and the pain and frustration in our lives stop hurting as much and help propel us further towards Godliness. Yes, we are God, blessed with all the attributes of God. Remember, we and God are one and God is greater!

24

PERSONAL AND IMPERSONAL

If God is All things, then it stands to reason that God is both personal and impersonal. Think of the personal as a microscope and the impersonal as a telescope. With a microscope you can get close and see things in exquisite detail, but you lose access to the big picture. With a telescope, you see the big picture at the expense of detail.

God is pure consciousness. This physical realm is a means of expression that God creates to define and refine God. There is no thing that is, that is not God. Think about this. You are God in God's most personal sense. If you wish to know God personally, know yourself. You are God, and God is greater. It is by knowing yourself that you gain access to the greater part of God. You gain access to All that is God, personal to impersonal and everything in between, through your personal relationship with yourself and God. This is how we bring our creative energy into this world, binding our personal conscious energy to the greater part of who we are, God. Everything that comes into physical manifestation is supported by God's impersonal energy. It is God's impersonal energy (big view) that supplies the matrix that tells everything what it is (lead to light) and what its characteristics are.

Ever wonder what keeps your heart beating? Think about all the things going on in your body that you don't have to consciously make happen. God takes care of it for us. God doesn't have to hover over us, personally telling our hearts to beat; God's impersonal energy handles it. God imbues you with the impersonal energy necessary to support your body in the beginning, programmed with the perfect flow of energy needed for this journey into self-realization, kind of like auto-pilot. Pay attention and you will be amazed to see God's impersonal energy supporting everything. Look within yourself and you will see and feel God's personal energy.

Think about how you love, the depth of your love, and think about how powerful your love can be. Think about what you will and can do for someone you love. Love can move mountains. With all the time you have had to polish your ability to express love, and as powerful as that love is, understand that God has had time beyond time, infinite time, to hone and polish God's ability to express love. You *are* God and God's love for you is God's love of God. The depth and power of this love is beyond description. You have to experience it within yourself to understand it. Once you find God's most personal love within yourself and invite it in, it grows and grows. It starts melting away any discordant energy and filling the empty space with love and light. All you need to do is ask to be open to God's love. Let go and let God. As you find God within yourself, you begin to see God in everything and in everyone. You see God's selfless love in the most personal loving sense, and you see God's impersonal energy powering and supporting everything on its journey to fulfillment.

We come into this life as babies with a selfless, rather impersonal understanding of who we are. As we gain experience, our sense of self begins to move away from our selfless impersonal understanding we came with towards a more self-centered personal identity, giving us more creative strengths. Our physical bodies, and the dynamic movement of the energy of the cosmos (astrology maps this energy), is designed to bring us from an innocent, impersonal childlike understanding at birth to a more self-centered and personal identity as we grow and mature. At mid-life our bodies are designed to begin the process of balancing our conscious focus back to the grander, more impersonal understanding of the big picture, that of Creators, only now we possess the understanding that comes from expressing God's selfless impersonal energy (that of the Creator) through our now developed sense of self (our I am) via our experience as created manifested beings. What set Jesus apart from mere mortals was that he completed the process, returning to the selfless state that we are all born in. This is what being born again really means: returning to the virginal state of conscious clarity we were all born with.

You will be amazed at the wellspring of support that envelops you, as it did Jesus, on every level of your very being. It helps to remember that while you are being supported top to bottom by God, and All that is, God's impersonal conscious energy does not bend to your personal agenda, and it is you who must learn to work within the power band that your connection to God's creative matrix gives you. Learning to be still, go within, and observe your conscious energy (thoughts and feelings) will help you to synchronize your personal energy with God's omnipotent, omnipresent impersonal energy that animates everything.

Gaining our sense of self (our I am) is much like a day at the all-you-can-eat buffet. You're there to put on conscious weight, and for the most part, it is a fulfilling and pleasurable experience. What made Jesus special was that once he gained his conscious weight (his I am), he stopped going back for seconds and thirds and began the process of exercising any excess aspects of his self-centered identity that blocked his conscious connection to creation (God), allowing him to be born again into his childlike (virginal) state of oneness with God and All of creation.

25

BALANCE

The relative dynamics that power everything from light to lead requires that the defined opposing properties find balance in order to be expressed and defined in a creative manner. Balance plays a big role in creation, supporting the process of expressing energy, defining energy, and refining energy. We are here to express God's selfless conscious energy in a self-centered defined manner, giving each and every one of us our unique identity and connection to God. Our conscious connection to the matrix at birth balances our conscious perspective close to the selfless impersonal side of energy (God) and supports us as we gain experience, moving our focus into a more self-centered perspective.

Our alignment to the matrix supports the timing of the maturation of our bodies and the physiological and psychological shifts our bodies go through. For example, in men, the decrease in testosterone that occurs as they age is meant to happen, giving them access to their intuitive energy and allowing for a shift in their conscious flow of energy to a more grounding, selfless perspective. Women's decrease in estrogen as they mature is also meant to happen and supports women in moving their intuitive energy's balance towards their intellectual grounding side. This shift in our conscious flow of energy, as we grow from birth to maturity, aids us in becoming one with God, progressing from young children into a grander defined sense of self.

There are two defined aspects of who we are: the eternal, infinite, selfless side of who we are that has access to the wisdom of the big picture, and the finite, self-centered vehicle that expresses and defines our infinite energy as it gets filtered through our ego. The people who achieve the most tend to be the most self-centered among us. The reason for this is because their conscious energy is finely tuned into what they want, allowing them to express a more defined energy. Because they are so strongly focused on what they want, they tend to overlook the effects their energy has on the big picture and others and create imbalances because of their ignorance of everything but what they want.

Conversely, the more selfless among us would avoid the imbalances created by the self-centered, but selfless individuals tend to lack the self-centered drive to accomplish the really big stuff. The trick is finding balance where we have access to the wisdom of the big picture and can blend that wisdom into a focused, defined plan of action, using the best of both worlds. Finding balance in our world can change conflict into constructive progress, moving from working against one another to working together towards a mutually beneficial goal, and creating a world more pleasant and productive for everyone. Relative dynamics has always, and will always, push and pull on our created reality, powering us along on our eternal quest for realization and refinement.

We come into this life as children balancing our conscious energy on the We (God) side of our identity. As we grow and gain experience, our balance moves towards the self-centered side of our identity, giving us a more defined sense of self (I am). At mid-life, we are designed to start clarifying our conscious energy and return to the childlike state into which we were born. The people who ride their higher selfless conscious energy as they grow older remain mentally sharp, emotionally open, and physically graceful, while those who choose to balance their conscious energy down in the lower self-centered realm of their created bodies will become closed-minded, intolerant, rigid, and childish as they separate from their higher, sustaining selfless energy. This life is all about gaining our I am and learning to balance that energy with our (God's) greater selfless connection to All that is, God.

It's all about balance.

26

L E T T I N G   G O

What made Jesus more than a mere mortal man and gave him access to all his extraordinary powers was his clarity. He gained his clarity by letting go of any and all negative thoughts and feelings that hindered the free flow of conscious energy between himself and God.

Jesus spent a great deal of time alone, away from distractions, allowing him to quietly observe and balance the thoughts and feelings that he entertained, letting go of any thoughts or feelings that blocked or distracted his highest conscious energy. The conscious pathway between Jesus the man and that greater part of himself, the Creator, had been cleared of any conscious clutter that might impede the optimum flow of energy between himself and God, giving him the wisdom and abilities that have had such a profound impact on the world. The energy that Jesus dealt with throughout his life was extremely powerful and would have been unbearable, even for him, if he had not had the ability to let go of the energy that was not of the highest, most loving frequency. We all have this energy flowing through us constantly. Masters like Jesus had to learn to manage a flow of energy that is remarkably more potent than mere mortals could tolerate.

There is a relative flow of energy that is non-stop and never-ending between God and each and every one of us. What we feel within ourselves is the flow of energy coming from the selfless side of who we are (God) flowing to our self-centered side and returning back to God to complete the circuit. What we feel within is the result of this energy as it cycles through our consciousness (our sense of who we think we are). What we feel as negative energy is the energy grinding on our conscious clutter.

If we take the time, we will notice that our thoughts and feelings are the face that we put on this energy. When we are angry, sad, frustrated, or frightened, we tend to fixate on the event that caused those feelings instead of going within to observe the energy that supports what we are feeling. Everything that we perceive to be reality is an expression of energy. Many see the energy as an illusion and the material world as real, when in truth this physical world is the illusion, a physical representation of energy being expressed, finite in nature with a defined shelf life. Rather, it is our inner conscious energy that is infinite, eternal, and transcends time and space and what comes with us when we are born and leaves once our finite body dies. This conscious energy is who we truly are, and it is our conscious understanding that we build upon as we experience life.

Jesus became the great master that he was by taking the time and making the effort to be still, go within, and ask how the conscious energy he was entertaining served him. By letting go of the thoughts and feelings that did not vibrate at the highest rate of joy, love, and gratitude, he clarified his conscious pathway between himself and the greater part of who we are, God. Jesus was a spiritual luminary because of his clarity and his ability to access conscious energy greater than himself. This is the connection between the Me side of who we are with all of God's omnipotent, omnipresent awareness that inspires, informs, and supports us and All that is. Jesus' virginal birth occurred at the point when he set aside his self-centered perspective that impeded the conscious flow of energy between Jesus and All that is, God.

The debate about whether Jesus was God or man can be answered with this knowledge. Jesus said that the things he did, we will do, and greater. He made this statement knowing who we are and our connection to God and All that is. We are children of God, created in God's conscious image. We are expressing our conscious energy in a self-centered manner as man in our journey to develop our I am, and we are meant to refine the energy we are expressing which, when properly balanced, will bring us back to the point where we regain access to our omnipotent, omnipresent connection to God and All that is. What made Jesus appear special was the fact that he completed the cycle of going from a perspective of being one with God, walked the earth as man, and refined his conscious energy, returning him to the point of conscious clarity that he had before taking on all the conscious information that gave him his sense of self (his I am).

Have you noticed that enlightened masters who appear from time to time have certain commonalities? They tend to spend a fair amount of time off by themselves being still. They talk about letting go of negative thoughts and feelings and balancing conscious energy on the higher vibrational end of joy, gratitude, and love. Letting go of thoughts and feelings that don't feel right and don't serve your highest expression will enlighten you, making your Adventure more pleasant and fruitful. It's the path that Jesus and all great masters take. It's well marked; all that is required is desire.

27

ENLIGHTENMENT

What does it mean to be enlightened? Is it simply being really smart? Is there a school you can go to for enlightenment? If you want to bring light into a room, do you add something to the equation or do you simply raise the blinds that are blocking the light? You can't *think* your way to enlightenment. You are the light, the self connected to the selfless, the Me connected to the We. You are God at God's most personal expression, connected consciously to All that is, the greater part of God that Jesus spoke of. Becoming enlightened bridges the Me aspect of who you are with the We, or greater part of who you are. The light has always been there. You are that light. You come into this world well connected to your inner light, and begin placing information about who you think you are and what your reality is in between your sense of self (your I am) and your light (God), creating layers of consciousness that veil your connection to your source of God's sustaining energy.

It is the unprocessed conscious energy we don't eliminate that obscures our connection to our inner light. Much like a silk scarf (veil), this conscious clutter doesn't block the light, it just filters it. As we live our lives, we tend to constantly add layer upon layer of this conscious clutter, filtering out more and more light. The light never leaves or becomes weaker, it just gets obscured by all the conscious silk. Part of the problem is that silk is pleasing to the touch, masking its obstructive properties, and you know how pleasant a silk scarf feels on the skin.

After carrying our conscious clutter for so long, it becomes somewhat comfortable, and letting go seems like an unpleasant experience. As you begin to monitor your conscious energy and exercise aspects that don't serve your highest expression, you will notice an increase in your flow of conscious energy. You will begin to feel deeper and access a newfound energy and the wisdom that comes with this increased energy.

Your increased flow of energy will tend to grind on your conscious clutter with more intensity, which can at times be uncomfortable, but the increase in the flow of energy brings about an increase in wisdom and inner strength. Just let go, let God, pay attention, and be amazed.

Dynamics of Creation

28

E N E R G Y

What animates this physical realm? What makes the planets spin? What makes our hearts beat? Where does the energy come from and who makes it? God? If it's God who makes it, then how? If God is All there is, the beginning and the end, then ordering out for additional materials is out of the question. God can't call and have a generator dropped off. And what about extension cords? Energy is conceived by God, created of God, and animates God, allowing God to express and experience God. Everything is done in house. But how?

Energy comes from the interaction of two opposing forces. The symbol for Yin and Yang represents this energy. Remember that God is the beginning and the end. That means that everything that is, is God. This is important. If God is everything, this would mean that God is omnipotent and God's power would be in everything because God *is* everything. If God is everything, then it makes sense that God is also omnipresent. If God is All there is, then God has to always be present, in everything and every moment. Take a moment and reflect on the meaning of this simple truth.

If God is All there is, then it makes sense that God has had to create the energy that animates this Adventure. This has been done by separating God's conscious energy into its two distinct qualities, thought (+) and feeling (-). Thought is outgoing, masculine, intellectual, positively charged conscious energy. Feeling is receptive, feminine, intuitive, negatively charged grounding conscious energy. The story of Adam and Lilith describes this energy in direct opposition to one another.

Think of God as a circle divided in two equal portions, one half being positive, masculine, outgoing energy, and the other half being negative, feminine, receptive energy. With both halves being of equal opposing energy, all they can do is push on one another without anything to show for it. (Kinda sounds like too many of our relationships!)

Now, take a small amount of God's positive energy and place it into the negative half (Adam's rib), and take a small amount of God's negative energy and place it in the positive half (thanks for the nipples, Eve). The Yin and Yang sign symbolizes this exchange of energy. The white dot in the black half symbolizes Adam's rib, or thought, being injected into Eve's intuitive receptive energy and the black dot in the white half represents the reaction that comes from the positive energy of Adam being injected into the receptivity of Eve – Creation! Now instead of two opposing forces, you have two polar opposites working in perfect synchronistic union with one another. Both aspects of God can understand and empathize with the other, allowing the two halves to combine their energy and creating that which powers everything from pure thought, lead to light.

If you take the time to observe, you will marvel at this blending of masculine and feminine energy in everything. The best place to start looking is yourself. That's right, you! Men bring this energy into their Adventure by thinking first; these thoughts then raise feelings within. At this point, the wise man balances his thoughts with his feelings, giving him information as to the correctness of the thoughts he is entertaining at that moment. This comes from continual monitoring of one's thoughts and feelings. It is an exercising of one's intellect and emotions that builds strength and eliminates useless conscious weight, producing a more graceful, agile, and fit self.

Women bring this energy into their Adventure by feeling first; these feelings then raise thoughts within. At this point, the wise woman balances her feelings with her thoughts, giving her the correct information about that moment. This comes from continual monitoring of one's feelings and thoughts, an exercising of one's emotions and intellect that builds strength and eliminates useless weight, producing a more beautiful, graceful, and fit self.

Positive feelings create positive thoughts, negative feelings create negative thoughts. Learning to keep one's focus in the moment is important, for it is in the moment (right here, right now) that everything is created and maintained. When God said let there be light, it was in that moment that light was created. Not yesterday or tomorrow. Time is a beautiful illusion created to allow God and us to create consciously and then experience the effects of that which we have created in a timely manner. Without time, we would feel the effects of our thoughts and feelings instantly, and would find our expressions of consciousness limited by the immediate results of our actions being imposed upon us. It is time that allows us to create karma, experience the effects of what we have created, and consciously exercise our thoughts and feelings, raising our awareness to its highest level of expression.

Men's energy is intelligent and masculine, supported by intuitive and feminine energy. Women's energy is intuitive and feminine, supported by intelligent and masculine energy. Look at people you know and you will see this blending of energy to lesser or greater degrees — physically, mentally, emotionally, and spiritually. Think about it: a man with no intuitive feelings, pure intellectual energy without being balanced by its polar opposite, is like a battery with two positive terminals. A man with no feelings would lack the ability to discern the correctness of the thoughts he was entertaining, making him more beast than man. A woman with no intellectual energy to balance her intuitive energy would be one big ball of emotions, unable to direct her energy outside of herself.

The blending of masculine and feminine energy gives each individual their unique identity, allowing him or her to experience and express the energy that embodies who they truly are. Without exception, each individual has within them all the ingredients — physical, mental, emotional, and spiritual — to achieve perfect expression of self. Think of yourself as perfection wrapped in poop. It is the poop in your life that nourishes your Adventure and allows you to grow. If you find yourself standing in poop, understand that stewing on your problems and placing blame just draws flies. It is only when you stop judging, roll up your sleeves, and till the poop into the soil of your life that the flies and stink are replaced with the growth and fulfillment that balance brings.

Understand that your life is a manifestation of the energy that is truly you. The fastest way to change your life is to change the way you think and feel about your life. When you feel strongly about something, your thoughts blend with your emotions and send out vibratory energy that attracts and returns to you energy of corresponding vibration, and the circumstances and events that these vibrations attract, creating your reality. There truly are no coincidences. Pay attention!

Changing habits that have developed over a lifetime can be a challenge. A head-on frontal assault typically will leave you exhausted and frustrated. Diet would be a good example. You feel an emptiness that you fill with food, which temporarily fills the void but doesn't cure the emptiness. So, you eat more, which causes you to gain weight. You look at yourself in the mirror and, upon seeing the effects of your overeating, you go on a diet, which causes you to struggle with your emptiness that started the whole mess you are in. You hold out for a while, but your emptiness gets the better of you and the cycle starts again. Your best way out of this is not to struggle with your emptiness but observe how it feels. When you eat food, pay attention to how it makes you feel and how long that feeling lasts. Asking the question "Will a cup of yogurt or fruit feel better than filling yourself with cookies and ice cream?" raises the conversation from your stomach into your consciousness. Simply moving your focus from your struggle with food to observing what effects that struggle has on you, the eternal being within your body, will move the energy supporting this struggle up away from it, causing it to weaken, giving you more control of the process.

Let go of your struggle; stop judging yourself for behavior that does not serve your highest expression. Move your focus 180 degrees from the self-centered realm of effects to the conscious realm of cause, where everything that is, is created and maintained. Your negative thoughts and feelings about yourself and others create discordant vibrations and unsettle your mental, physical, emotional, and spiritual equilibrium.

Learn to step out of your judgments and observe your behavior. See how your actions make you feel and how your actions affect those around you and your interactions with them. How your feeling body resonates will tell you the correctness of the conscious energy that you are entertaining. If it doesn't feel right, you know to make adjustments. Don't go to war with yourself by judging your behavior harshly; that hasn't worked. Just observe without judgment. As you pay attention to your vibrational energy (thoughts and feelings), the correct focus of energy will become apparent.

When you first start listening to your little voice (your thoughts and feelings), it may not seem to be speaking very much, very loud, or at all. Yet your little voice has always been speaking to you, is speaking right now, and will keep giving you the correct information at every moment of your life, if only you learn to listen. This pure, selfless energy is ever present and remains your perpetual, perfect link to the Allness of God. It is right here, right now. It always has been and always will be. It is in the moment that is right here and right now that this perfect energy resides. Learn to be still and know this perfect energy. The more time (energy) you invest in this perfect energy, the more you will understand it and its many applications. In doing so, you will become truly powerful – truly Christ-like.

29

R E L A T I V E   D Y N A M I C S

Reality is, needless to say, complex: there is a whole lot of stuff being expressed, from light to lead and everything in between. Is there one simple dynamic that creates, sustains, and empowers what we view as reality? Something that would help us understand the omnipotent, omnipresent part of God? Looking at the occurrence that began God's and our Adventure is the simplest place to start, given that the energy that we're looking to understand was at its simplest expression in the beginning.

First, understanding the eternal part of the equation is helpful. The eternal aspect of God that has always existed is selfless receptive awareness. It has always been aware but had no thing to be aware of. What created the very first spark that ignited reality was God turning in on God. This was the point where the selfless became self-aware. So, what are the dynamics involved?

Selfless awareness is receptive in nature and transcends time and space. Think of a membrane or a calm body of water capable of creating expressions of energy (ripples) but requiring outgoing energy (a rock) to initiate the process. This represents the sacred feminine, or Eve aspect of creation. In the Bible, Eve (the receptive side of creation) felt the desire to understand relative dynamics and experience the growth that would come with that understanding but, being receptive in nature, lacked the ability to initiate the process – enter Adam.

Adam represents positive outgoing energy, the polar opposite quality of Eve. Understand that Adam and Eve represent the two dynamics involved in creation yet are one. The Yin and the Yang sign illustrates this relative dynamic. You start with the circle. This represents that which is to be created. The circle is separated into its two opposing properties, the desire and the definition of the desire. Black represents negatively charged receptive energy (the desire) and white represents positively charged outgoing energy (the desire defined). At this point there are two halves of the whole. One is receptive and grounding and one is outgoing and positively charged. This is the Adam and Lilith phase, in which all the two opposing forces can do is push on one another. Adam and Lilith are equal, with Adam being outgoing energy and Lilith being receptive energy. When combined, Adam's energy fills Lilith's equal receptive energy, cancelling out Lilith, cancelling out the energy, and yielding no viable expression of the two combined energies. The story about Adam and Eve explains the next step in the process of the relative dynamics involved in creation.

Next, God takes one of Adam's ribs and gives it to Eve. This represents the thought (blueprint) of what could be being injected onto the receptivity of the feminine receptive, grounding energy (Eve). What was deleted from the story was the fact that Eve gave Adam something in return. Ever wonder why men have nipples? Okay, stop laughing. Men's nipples are representative of the feminine energy that was returned to Adam as the response to information sent with the rib, which balances every man's energy just as masculine energy balances women. Eve just got Adam's message (the rib), which created vibrational energy that, like a rock being thrown into a calm pond, produced energy. Eve's gift to Adam (the set of nipples) was the completion of the circuit returning back to Adam, that which is desired.

The process begins with the feeling, the desire to create some thing. This is Eve wanting the apple. Eve nudges Adam and expresses the desire for Adam to pick the apple (begin the relative process of creation). This creates the relative vibrational energy that supports the process of creation (the matrix). Eve represents desire and the receptive, grounding side of the equation; Adam represents the desire defined and outgoing, positively charged energy.

Or, think of Adam as the pitcher and Eve as the catcher. Eve expresses her desire (gives Adam the sign to throw a fastball). The outgoing energy of Adam's pitch hits Eve's mitt (receptive energy), inducing a vibrational splash that creates a matrix representative of Adam's and Eve's combined energy, which will attract and support a finite expression of the infinite energy. Creation occurs when the circuit becomes complete and releases the relative energy that comes from the blending of relative opposites.

Consider the structure of a triangle. The first thing you will notice will be the three sides that make up the triangle. Closer inspection shows that there are two more elements, the empty space within the triangle and the empty space surrounding it. The space within the triangle represents our infinite conscious awareness. The space outside the triangle represents God's omnipresent, omnipotent infinite conscious awareness. Can you see the relative dynamics of our infinite conscious connection to God? The empty space represents God's and our eternal state of infinite conscious awareness. The triangle represents the structure used to create and bring forth infinite conscious energy. The empty space within the triangle represents God's and our infinite sense of self, our I am, where creation is originated. The empty space outside the triangle represents God's selfless infinite awareness, where creation is supported and brought to its perfect expression. The triangle represents the structure that binds the desire (where creation originates) to the defined expression in its perfect state of expression (the finished product).

There are three sides of a triangle. The first side represents the desire to create. The second side of the triangle represents the desire being defined. The third side that completes the triangle and lends it its structural strength is the blending of the desire and the desire defined, creating the perfect expression of the two combined forces. This relative creative process is what defines everything that ever has and ever will be defined and energizes every moment of creation and the creations being expressed within that moment. Understanding the simple dynamics behind this eternal truth enables us to step up into the conscious realm of creation and co-create with God and All that is as our great Adventure of discovery unfolds.

30

R E L A T I V E   E X I S T E N C E

Relative existence is the means by which God expresses, defines, and refines. To express, there must be a point of reference from which to express. To define something, you must also know what it is not. This is a relative exercise. This relative exercise is what refines. By shifting focus from what it is to what it is not, we refine the quality of our focus until all that remains is its true essence. Everything that comes into this physical, three-dimensional realm comes supported by relative energy. Subjective energy (desire) that is expressed into this three-dimensional realm is the matrix that holds this Adventure together.

Science now knows that nothing is truly solid, but what science has not yet discovered is what holds all of this seemingly solid stuff together. The same energy that guides and animates the planets is what guides and animates our bodies and everything in this three-dimensional relative realm. The subjective energy supports the wish fulfilled (the ideal in its state of finished perfection), while its relative opposite, objective energy, supports the process of refinement and fulfillment in this physical realm. As the relative process of refinement progresses, the refined energy of this objective realm is reflected and refined in the subjective realm, adding that refined energy to our (God's) true essence, our (God's) bag of tools.

As we refine our understanding, we raise our vibrational energy from what is not into what is, moving into a higher and finer range of understanding of truth. An understanding wherein relative energy can continue to propel us to even higher levels of understanding, elevating us to a lighter and brighter energy level. This entire Adventure is based on relative dynamics. It is dark that defines light, in that defines out, and up that defines down. We would have no understanding of light if all there was were light. It would just be the state you were experiencing and, having nothing to compare it to, it would have little meaning. It is only when this frightening polar opposite of light descends upon it or consumes it when light can truly be seen for what it is.

In a state of knowing only God, knowing only God's love and God's light, we had no idea what God, God's love, or God's light was. We had no point of reference. It was our Fall into relative existence that gave us our understanding of God, God's love, and God's light. As we exercise aspects of self that don't serve us, we peel away the veil (layers of untruth), leaving only God's love, God's light, and God's truth, raising our understanding and giving us more energy to advance to a higher, more rewarding level of existence.

31

S U B J E C T I V E   S T A T E

A subjective state is a state of being where reality (focus) is subject to the creative powers of the force from which it originates, without any external (or internal) forces interacting to distort or alter it. A subjective state is a passive state, a sleep state in the sense that this state requires only desire, and the focus that comes from that desire. This state is the water phase of the water and blood spoken of in the Bible. The objectified state represents the blood in which the desire is brought into manifestation.

When desire becomes so strong and becomes defined as the wish fulfilled, the joy that comes with this realization acts as a catalyst, exciting all that is wished for into a "Big Bang" (Big Orgasm), creating the conscious matrix (energy) required for bringing into physical existence all the necessary ingredients for the fulfillment of that which is desired. It is the faithful adherence to the ideal of the wish fulfilled that nourishes the matrix that supports the fulfillment of the desire. All that is needed now is to be aware of the energy that animates the fulfillment of the wish desired, so that proper action can be taken as the energy of the matrix settles into the physical realm. This is turning water into blood. Taking desire and bringing it to fruition. Bringing conscious subjective desire into this physical objective realm where we can work with and observe the effects of consciousness, allowing us to evolve into wiser, more powerful children of God, just like God.

Science is yet to realize that everything that is comes from this subjective state of no thingness (consciousness) and is given its unique qualities (vibrational energy) through this subjective state of awareness. Think of the subjective state as the negative (film) and this objective realm as the picture. As long as the image of the negative stays sharp and focused (well-defined image of the wish fulfilled), the picture develops into the manifestation of that which is desired. It is holding the subjective image of the wish fulfilled that binds together what we see as the real world. In truth, this physical world (realm) is the symptom (the created state), and the realm of thought (consciousness) is the cause (the Creator). As we come to this realization, we begin to create consciously with our imaginations instead of trying to impose our will upon the physical world. We begin to move into our authentic power as true Creators, created in God's conscious image.

32

OBJECTIVE STATE

The objective state of consciousness is the state in which that which is defined in the subjective state is refined and brought to its perfect expression. The objective state allows external energies to interact with the creative energies of subjective creation. Think of it as having a great concept and sitting down with a group of trusted friends with different points of view (perspectives). You bat the concept around from all conceivable viewpoints. Through this process, the weak and imbalanced aspects are exposed. It can be painful and frightening if the process is not understood for what it is. But if you stay true to the process, you begin to see all aspects of your concept that don't serve its perfect expression, making refinement easier.

In order for this process to be successful, the subjective image of the wish fulfilled (the finished product) must be faithfully maintained, much like a blueprint that must be clear and defined, providing the structural matrix on which creation can be built. This process also reveals the truth, bringing forth the highest, most effective means of conscious expression. This process is to consciousness what food is to the body. The thoughts and feelings we entertain attract vibrational energy that is aligned to our own vibrational frequency, allowing for the expression of our consciousness in this physical realm where we can observe and understand our creative energy as we feel the effects of our creations, allowing for conscious growth.

Understanding the simple dynamics of consciousness raises your awareness closer to the creative vibrational realm of Heaven. Everything of meaning that is brought into the objective realm of consciousness is created and sustained in this high vibrational realm. This subjective energy is the matrix that our physical realm is sustained by. Light is light because of God's understanding of the principles of Creation, and the subjective application of these principles upon the matrix that supports and animates our physical existence. The subjective realm is the cause, and the physical realm is the effect. The fastest way to change your life is to change the way you think about it. Sound crazy? Think about it. Before you take a step, you think about making that step. Before you eat, you think about it; without exception, all action is preceded by a thought. It is our thoughts that animate our Adventure, it is our feelings about our thoughts that create our reality.

As we learn to maintain an unwavering subjective view of that which we desire to create, our created objective world becomes more productive and meaningful. As we gain wisdom about the relative dynamics involved in this objective world, we learn that balancing the energy is much easier and far more effective, being consciously aware and in the moment, rather than living in the pain of the past or the anxiety of the future.

33

V I B R A T I O N

If everything comes from the same thing (God), and lead and light come from the same source, what gives them their unique qualities? Vibration! Everything has its own unique identity that is associated with its rate of vibration. Change the rate that something vibrates, and you change its characteristics. There is nothing that is brought into physical manifestation that cannot be manipulated. Its expression can be changed by raising or lowering its rate of vibration. This is done by changing the energy that supports it.

Think of our physical realm as a giant diaphragm, like a speaker. The sound that comes from the speaker is the physical representation of the energy being sent to the speaker. Change the energy received by the speaker and the music changes. Raise the energy and you get a finely tuned melody, lower the energy and you get a discordant noise, or somewhere in between, depending on the energy expressed.

We are all constantly injecting our energy onto the eternal diaphragm of this relative realm. Many of us wield our energy out of ignorance of the law and cannot understand how a loving God could allow such imbalances to be visited upon us. The truth of the matter is that the energy you put into this physical realm returns to you as the physical manifestation known as your life.

If you don't like certain aspects of your life, change the way you think and feel about them. As you learn to raise your energy to a higher vibrational level, you will begin to notice changes. The first thing you notice, if you're paying attention, is that you feel better physically when your energy is up. Pay attention to your feeling body; it is what keeps you informed as to the nature of the energy you are processing. Negative energy causes dis-ease; your heart beats hard, your body tightens up, and your energy drops from your heart to the pit of your stomach. It throws your body out of sync with the energy that is you. This uncomfortable phenomenon hinders your performance and can cause disease in your physical body.

It is also important to know that feeling a certain way about something is like throwing a rock into a still pond. The energy ripples out on the matrix that supports our Adventure, reaches the outer shores of our (God's) consciousness, and ripples back to us in the form of events and people in our lives. You could call it karma. If you wish to raise the quality of your Adventure, raise the quality of your thoughts. Thoughts are things. There is no action, no thing, that comes into physical being without the thought to conceive it and the emotion that acts as the catalyst to bring it to realization.

Send out discordant energy and it will manifest as an experience of like energy. Raise your vibrational energy about a given aspect of your life, and watch it evolve into a higher expression of your reality. Change how you think and feel about something, and watch it transform. For better or worse, it is the law. Use it wisely!

34

C R E A T I V E   E V O L U T I O N

God creates in an evolutionary way, and God evolves in a creative manner. The first step in creating is to have a hunger, to feel a need or desire. Second, God must define that desire — what is it? Third, God must define the feeling God would have were the desire fulfilled. This is important because this feeling of the wish fulfilled is the catalyst that sets the creative process in motion. Holding a well-defined image of that which is desired, viewed in its state of fulfillment, is the blueprint. The joy (excitement) God would experience from having the desire fulfilled is the catalyst that starts and maintains the creative evolution into that which is desired.

Faith is maintaining a belief that is yet to be supported by the facts, the belief in something that has not manifested into being. Faith is focused subjective energy that supports the energy matrix which, in turn, supports and energizes this three-dimensional realm we live in. The energy (thoughts) we (God) put into our world [what we (God) think and how we (God) feel about it] sends out vibrations that by the law of attraction finds and returns into our environment the vibrational energy that will attract that which is desired. God's subjective focus (the wish fulfilled) is the matrix that supports this three-dimensional objective realm. As long as the subjective picture is maintained (faith), the matrix that supports the fulfillment of the wish desired remains active. Pay attention and allow the wish to be fulfilled.

35

THE "BIG BANG"
(THE BIG ORGASM)

How reality as we know it came into being is a hotly debated topic. Science, however, is yet to come up with a theory that starts from no thing. Common sense requires that reality had to start from a state of no thingness, which raises the question, what exactly is no thing, and how can some thing (this finite realm) come from it?

First, we must understand the eternal side of the equation. The aspect of God that is eternal and has always existed is selfless awareness. God has always been aware but had no thing to be aware of. Then what happened to make God self-aware? Selfless awareness has always had a vibrational frequency but was unable to express the undefined state of selfless awareness without any relative information or point of reference to define it. When this selfless energy turned in on itself, it caused a vibrational variance, a shift in the frequency (lowering the frequency) that became self-evident, giving God a relative point of reference, or God's I am.

God has been expressing, defining, and refining God's conscious energy for a really long time. There have been countless "Big Bangs" that have brought God's infinite conscious energy to the point of expression that we now see as our reality. Time and space are finite expressions of God's infinite conscious energy that God created as a means to define and refine understanding on God's quest to know God.

What science calls the "Big Bang," and the resulting expression of energy we see as our reality, comes from the relative dynamics that were established when God's selfless awareness turned 180 degrees in on itself and became self-aware. God began balancing selfless with self-centered, in with out, expressing the relative energy that became self-evident with each new expression and expanding God's own knowledge as Creator. God spent a fair amount of effort (time would be a good word to use to express the effort God put into knowing God's creative abilities, but time and space were yet to be defined and established as a means of expression, so "effort" is most apt) gaining understanding of God's infinite conscious character and God's creative abilities as they became self-evident.

The story of Genesis explains more than the physical creation of this universe. Consider the order of what was created; you will notice that creation started with energy at the highest vibrational rate of infinite consciousness (the first light was not physical) and was vibrationally lowered step by step into the finite realm of physical expression. Prior to the creation of our current expressed finite reality, God has experienced lots of Adventures into the expressed vibrational energy that God has learned to create, starting with pure infinite energy and working down the vibrational scale into physical light and sound (can you imagine the spectacular light shows God has expressed throughout time?). As God has gained experience and expanded God's perspective (focus), what could be expressed has become more complex and diversified with the practical knowledge that God has gained from the experience of creating. God's and our purpose for being is to express our conscious energy, to define that energy, and to refine our defined conscious energy to its highest expression.

36

T I M E   A N D   S P A C E

Time and space became self-evident out of the necessity to allow God to define the unique qualities of God's conscious energy, not as one, but as a multitude of unique expressions, each with its own qualities which required separation and space to define that which was being defined. Space-time was created to accommodate the movement and synchronistic interactions of conscious energy as it was expressed in the finite realm, allowing God to enlarge God's understanding and expand conscious evolution.

If you think about it, everything that has ever happened or been created happened and was created *in the moment*. The eternal infinite truth of who God and we are transcends time and space and can be viewed as the eternal moment with God's first realization of self (God's I am), as the small grain of consciousness that caused God's selfless eternal awareness to begin to add layer upon layer of conscious energy. Much like the development of a pearl, it built up to the point that God and we are presently experiencing. You don't have to go back in time to revisit God's first realization of self. It exists in the moment, as does everything in between this present moment and God's awakening. You just have to be capable of going deeper into consciousness, which requires clarity and living in the moment.

The first thing that happens with a "Big Bang" (creation) is that the image of that which is to be created is consciously expressed in its final state of completion, which represents the positive charge needed to energize that which is to be expressed. Expressing the higher vibrational energy we associate with joy, gratitude, and love creates the receptive grounding energy which, when blended with the image of the completed expression, creates a conscious matrix (blueprint) that attracts and energizes the finite materials needed for completion of the creative process.

Space supports the finite expressions we are now experiencing, allowing God, and us, to define conscious energy with a hands-on experience, much like an artist uses a canvas to express their infinite conscious energy. Space is God's canvas. Time is God's paint brush. Time brings movement and definition to that which is created, allowing God to witness the creative process in a timely manner that can be observed and measured as it unfolds, giving God and us an enhanced understanding of the dynamics involved. Time allows for more than one defined creation to utilize the same space, defining synchronicity and rhythm. Time also allows for the dynamics of karma to mete out the effects of conscious energy in a timely manner, allowing for more rapid growth and understanding of God's and our creative abilities.

37

A S T R O L O G Y   A N D   A S T R O N O M Y

In the past, astrology and astronomy were studied together. Astronomy is the study of the physical universe and astrology is the study of that which animates the universe. Before there was matter in this three-dimensional realm, there was the energy that animates it. The first thing that came into objective reality was the energy that animates this objective three-dimensional realm. It is this subjective energy (everything is subject to its influence/power) that binds everything together in this physical realm, from the subatomic to the galactic. It gives everything its proper place in time and space. As this energy moves the universe, it animates matter, not only giving it its physical identity but also supporting its intake and exchange of energy with everything that comes into our realm of experience. This energy has imprinted on it every ingredient for the complete, perfect fulfillment of the wish desired.

Before the "Big Bang" (and there have been many), while we (God) were in our natural state of subjective consciousness, we (God) thought about all we (God) were, all we (God) had become, and with all that information, dwelt on what we (God) desired to become. From these thoughts, we (God) found our next perfect expression of self and imagined it in its highest, brightest, most perfect expression (the last scene of the play). The thought of the wish fulfilled held in subjective focus (calm subjective state) was struck with the energy of the joy of the wish fulfilled. This burst of joyful energy injected into the calm subjective image of the wish fulfilled created ripples of energy that burst forth, much like the ripples of energy that occur when a rock is thrown into a calm pool of water. This is the same effect embodied in the words "let there be light." This is the matrix that holds our material world together, supports light being light, air being air, water being water, lead being lead, and you being you.

The energy that this physical realm rides upon is much like a train riding on rails. The destination is predetermined. You can get off the train and take diversionary adventures but you need to stay on the track (your astrological energy that guides and supports your journey towards fulfillment). When people get too involved in the pursuits of the ego (self-centered gratification), they move away from the selfless energy that supports them. Have you noticed that some people begin to lose their physical and mental faculties as they age while others remain youthful and sharp? This is why.

Our alignment to the planets at our conception, fine-tuned by the time of our birth, gives each of us our unique connection to the matrix that animates our reality and our lives. As time and space move across our infinite point of focus in the moment we see as reality, the movement of the matrix causes our bodies to grow and mature on a physical level and supports our conscious growth on the higher levels of energy. The movement of the matrix affects the weather, the instinctual behavior of animals, the growth patterns of plant life, the sun's projection of energy, and much more. Your body's physiology along with your conscious makeup is guided by the matrix from birth until death.

Understanding the fundamentals of astrology allows for a more enlightened and productive Adventure. Contrary to the common misconception, astrology can't tell you what will make you happy in your life, but it can inform you of your particular alignment to the matrix and the energy involved. When seers and prophets look into the future, they are not looking at events yet to happen but rather at the alignment of the energy of the matrix at a given point in time and space. Astrology in it truest form is the study of the energy that animates the universe.

The matrix links the Creator, and the moment of creation, to the finished defined creation and acts as the blueprint that attracts the raw materials and supports their expression into physical matter. The matrix essentially links the beginning of creation to its ultimate end. Physical matter (our reality) rides on this energy, and this energy is what allows gravity to push and pull the planets, moving the cosmos and creating the energy to animate this Adventure we call life. As the planets move through time and space guided by the matrix, their continually changing alignments create the energy that we feel within ourselves in our daily lives that astrologers can read, giving us understanding as to the energy that supports us at any given point in our lives. Knowing where and when we were born gives astrologers access to the astrological energy that expresses each of our individual genetic energy, giving each of us our unique character. A volume of books could be written on this as mankind has only scratched the surface of this very deep subject.

38

THE ADVENTURE

Most descriptions of God describe God as perfect. This is true, but what is perfection? Perfection is a state of being, but it is not static, nor is it a final destination. God has always had stuff to do and things to learn about in God's eternal quest to know God. This physical realm and many lighter realms, both physical and non-physical, exist as a means by which God expresses, defines, and refines God.

God is constantly growing. Always has and always will. That is what God does. That is God's purpose for being. God thrives on adventure, learning, and growing. Though it can be painful, it is also deeply rewarding and fun. And God loves fun.

What we call life is a very carefully scripted story set forth as a means by which God expresses, defines, and refines God. Remember, there is no thing that is, that is not God. We and God are one and God is greater. God is no thing (pure consciousness) and we are created in God's image. That thing you look at in the mirror and call you is your temple (your vehicle), allowing you to experience this objective realm.

Your body is your ride, allowing you to get about and experience whatever you choose to be conscious of, allowing you to grow and expand your awareness of self. Where we are, God once was, and where God is, we will be. We are God's children and as we grow and become greater, God is also growing and becoming greater. God's greatness will always be here to support us, no matter how great we become. And our potential, like God's, is limitless.

Every day when you wake up, take a minute to remember that All that is, God, is here right now to support you in your quest for understanding of self. God wrote this Great Adventure with the most perfect ending that God could imagine. God produces this Great Adventure with every ingredient necessary for its perfect expression and then directs it, keeping it on script as we progress on our journey of growth and self-realization. We are the actors and must know our lines and bring the expression of God (that is, us) to its highest expression. We memorize our lines by spending time every day asking for wisdom by going within (knock) and quietly listening to our thoughts and feelings for God's wisdom, which is constantly available, 24/7/365. Remember, God invented time and uses it to express, define, and refine us, but God also transcends time. God is always right here, right now, available to assist us every moment of our lives. What God desires most for us is our full and complete realization of self, for us to know ourselves as the children of God, endowed with all the blessings and attributes of divinity.

This thing we call life was lovingly conceived and is being perfectly supported by God to give us the perfect environment to explore ourselves and refine all the qualities we discover within ourselves. Remember what you get to keep doesn't fit in your purse or pocket. What we keep, and can never be taken from us, is our awareness of ourselves. We are pure consciousness clothed in physical bodies. What we take with us is our understanding, not that shiny car in the garage or all the gold in your safe. Use all the wonderful stuff that this physical world affords us, but remember that it is all here to assist us in expressing, defining and refining ourselves. When it has served its purpose, it always gets put back in the box. Enjoy all of it. Use it wisely and remember what is truly real and of value. Have a Great Adventure!

39

B A L A N C E

We come from a state of conscious oneness with All that is (God). We are here to gain our I am (sense of self). Oneness with God is the We side of who we are. The sense of self that we are here to develop. Our I am stands 180 degrees opposite from the We side of the equation. We start from a selfless state of oneness with God. Our Fall serves to compel us to gain our sense of self, but we are expected to return to that state of oneness with God. So what's the point? *Balance.*

When we were in our selfless innocent state of consciousness, our conscious energy was limited to our ability of relative understanding, which had no point of reference. Our Fall moved our point of reference from We (an inward perspective of oneness with God) to Me, where we viewed everything as separate and outside ourselves, God included – dichotomous perspectives that sit opposite each other. Our Fall shifted our perspective from selfless and impersonal to self-centered and personal.

Think of a board being used as a lever. If the fulcrum is at the selfless end of the board, there is no leverage for creation. Likewise, if the fulcrum is at the self-centered end of the board, there is no creative leverage. Understand that creation always starts with desire for that which is to be created. That desire comes from the self-focused side of consciousness, and when introduced to the selfless receptive side of consciousness, via thought blended with the feeling of the desire fulfilled, it precipitates the vibrational energy that creates the matrix that attracts and supports the physical manifestation. Having the ability to move our conscious fulcrum at will strengthens us as Creators.

Think of the selfless side of consciousness as a still pond and your self-centered side of consciousness as an arm holding a rock. The rock represents your desire, the arm's strength is your sense of self (your I am). The stronger your I am (sense of who you are), the bigger the rock you can handle, and the bigger splash you can make in the creative realm of consciousness. Everything comes from and is supported by a conscious matrix, so the stronger your sense of self, the greater your creative potential and the impact upon the matrix. This is what makes us greater than the Angels in Heaven. They have not had the experience necessary to gain their I am. They are yet to make the Fall that turns their focus from We (one with God and All that is) 180 degrees to the relative opposite side of the equation to gain their I am. Our ability to balance our conscious energy between our self-center and our selfless connection to God gives us potential greater than that of the Angels.

What about the most self-centered among us? They seem to be running the show, creating imbalances and generating an abundance of poop in the world – living high on the hog and leaving pig droppings everywhere. Remember that poop makes things grow, and we are here to grow. If it were not for these self-centered individuals, we would not be able to experience the most self-centered side of consciousness because our understanding of who we truly are would prevent us from becoming so imbalanced. The most self-centered individuals in the world create situations due to their ignorance that pull less self-centered people into the energy and circumstances of their making, allowing the less self-centered individuals to gain experience they would not have wanted to endure had it not been imposed upon them. Think about all of the wisdom you have gained over your lifetime that came from others' self-centered energy, causing you to have interactions and deal with circumstances that ultimately were not of your making. Someone else supplies the poop, and you get growth and the balance and understanding that comes from the experience.

We truly are eternal beings, and mankind is consciously spread all over the creative evolutionary wheel of existence. We start out innocent, and as we experience the many lives that we have lived, we evolve from a selfless state of innocent awareness to a self-centered point of reference. If we were all on the same page, our experiences would not create the diverse opportunities that this life's Adventure offers. The innocent new souls need the energy created by the self-centered to pull them down to a more self-centered level of consciousness, where they can begin to gain their sense of self. As we gain our self-center and begin our journey back into a selfless relationship with ourselves and God, we require poop to fuel that growth, and it is the most self-centered among us who create the most poop. We are meant to balance our energy as we evolve so that our self-centeredness does not obstruct our return to conscious oneness with God, and it is the process of going within and balancing our conscious energy that keeps us within reach of God's omnipresent, omnipotent sustenance.

Everything is relative, and it is God's and our ability to balance our conscious energy that gives us our abilities as Creators, created in God's conscious image.

40

F R E E   W I L L

What is will? Will comes from desire, and our will becomes stronger as we practice getting our way. Willpower comes from the self-centered side of consciousness and is what drives us to explore and expand our conscious awareness. Without self-centered drive, we would not have any desire to expand our awareness and would simply be selfless awareness with nothing to be aware of.

So how does the process of growth and conscious evolution work? First, we must realize that what we perceive to be reality is the result of lots of work, God's and ours, consciously expressing, defining, and refining God's conscious awareness. Each new realization expands awareness and opens up new possibilities and questions to be answered. This dynamic supports God's omnipresent, omnipotent eternal awareness. While God truly does understand everything that has been observed, each new observation expands God's ability to go deeper into the eternal question: "What are we capable of?" Experience has given God the wisdom to implement structure within this Adventure that allows for the movement of conscious energy, providing forward momentum to the evolution of understanding ourselves.

The moment in time and space when we are born gives us our own alignment to this energy that will support each of our unique lives. Our free will lies within the astrological structure that the moment of our birth gives us. The person you have chosen to be in this life came with defined strengths and challenges, designed to give you the growth necessary for your evolution towards understanding you and your connection to All that is, God. But remember that freedom walks hand in hand with responsibility. The more responsible we become, the more capable we are of experiencing what life brings us. If you compare your body to a vehicle, which it is, you can see that the car you drive has strengths and limitations. A corvette can go fast, handles like a dream on a windy road, but try hauling boulders or manure and you're in for a bad day. You can drive it off road, but will it survive intact? All vehicles have strengths and weaknesses. If we are wise we can experience life within the structure our vehicles (our bodies) afford us and have a productive Adventure.

The guidance that keeps us within our power comes from within, and we gain access to this wisdom by learning to still our thoughts and feelings: "be still and know I am." Our connection to God and All that is can always be felt in the moment. It is impossible for us to exist without this conscious connection to God and All that is, and it cannot be broken. Focusing outside ourselves, with our thoughts and feelings darting to and fro, forgetting to live in the moment conscious of what's going on within, impedes our connection to God and our power. Remember that we bring conscious awareness with us, and it is conscious awareness that we take when we leave this Adventure.

What is of the highest value lies within you, and it is that consciousness that dictates the quality of your Adventure. If you are angry, your vibrational energy (thoughts and feelings) will attract people and events that will allow you to express and experience this energy. The same goes for happy, sad, and everything in between. God gives us what we ask for, no matter what that is. If we ask for cake, or poop, God will oblige us, but understand that God does not listen to our words, God listens to our vibrational energy. God also speaks to us not in words but with vibrational energy. Stop waiting to hear God's voice. God is not a dude with a pair of lips that move when speaking to us. Think about it.

We are God, and God is greater. The truth does not support the notion of an old man in the sky who sits back, separate from us, watching and acting according to whether we have pleased or pissed him off. We and God are literally one, and we are connected consciously. Our true power lies within, and is greater than what lies within the body we see in the mirror. As we learn to go within, still our minds, and feel the energy within, we connect to a power far greater than ourselves. This wisdom has all the answers to every question we will ever have. When

Jesus said "My Father and I are one, and my Father is greater," he was misunderstood, actually saying that we and God are one, and God is greater. He was speaking of our conscious connection to All that is, God. As we strengthen our conscious connection with God, we gain wisdom that is greater than what is contained within our physical bodies, and we begin to become wiser since we now are receiving information and support from a source greater than ourselves. This added awareness broadens the options open to us and adds the power of the universe, and God's will, to our bag of conscious tools.

41

D E M O N S

What is a demon? Conventionally, the thought of them provokes ideas of fear and darkness, and we tend to spend a fair amount of time wrestling with them. So, what can be done to exorcise demons and expel them from our Adventure? The first step is to get to know the little buggers. In truth, they are not nearly as big or scary as they appear, once you look at them.

Demons feed on fear and ignorance and deeply fear the light. Demons know that once the light illuminates them, people can see that the only power demons have over us is the power that we give them. That is why demons are associated with darkness. They are deathly frightened of the light because they know that the light reveals the truth about their impotence. Fear empowers demons and ignorance feeds fear. The light of knowing illuminates ignorance, vanquishing demons' power. Any kind of dysfunction, disdain, or conflict is fueled by ignorance and driven by our demons.

If demons are not physical and possess no real power in this physical realm, why do they sometimes wield so much influence over us, and why are we always wrestling with them? The answer is relative. Remember that God is All there is, and we are God and God is greater. There is no free lunch, not for us or God. Relative dynamics power everything from the simplest thought and feeling to the greatest manifestation and everything in between.

Without the energy that comes from defining and separating the qualities of that which is to be brought forth, there would be no means to define anything. Light requires its polar opposite, dark, to define it. Up requires down, in requires out. Everything must be defined in this relative manner. It is the interaction of these relative opposites that fuel

God's and our evolution. Remember that we are consciously connected to God and All that is and the perpetual interaction of conscious energy fuels our Adventure. As we experience life, our experiences create conscious energy (conscious information catalogued in our intuitive feeling body in the form of thoughts and feelings).

The pain we feel from our demons comes from energy trying to work its way through conscious clutter. So, how do we exorcise our demons? The first thing is to learn that wrestling with them just makes us weaker and our demons stronger. Never wrestle with a demon. You both get dirty, and the demon likes it. The most effective way to tame a demon is to rise above the demon and the mess it represents. This is done by moving our conscious energy from the Me side of our conscious perspective to the We side. The Me side of our consciousness is what makes our potential greater than the Angels. We are more self-centered than the Angels and have the ability to venture farther from the We side of consciousness, giving us more conscious leverage and greater access to all of God's omnipotent, omnipresent power. But we must learn to clean up our conscious clutter as we go. Allowing us to utilize our unique conscious energy requires that we maintain a clear pathway between ourselves and God's omnipresent, omnipotent power.

Eliminating the conscious clutter that does not serve our highest interest opens up our conscious pathway to the power that animates us, our world, and everything in existence (God). This increased volume of creative energy can be focused on bringing more depth and meaning into your life and the lives of those you interact with. What we experience as demons is our energy being diffused and depleted by the unprocessed conscious clutter as our energy cycles between us and what supports and sustains us, God.

What made Jesus so great was the free flow of energy that circulated between him and God, unimpeded by his ego. What made Jesus greater than Solomon was that he, unlike Solomon, never stopped the process of refinement. In the story of Solomon, Solomon loses his powers and goes crazy after worshiping his wife's idols. This represents Solomon turning from his inner focus, and the continual process of refinement that gave him all his wisdom and power, to an outward focus on worldly gratification and the pleasures of the flesh. The conscious pathway between himself and God's creative force that he had spent his entire life opening up and making clear became clogged as he turned 180 degrees away from his inner light and chose to serve his ego rather than his higher energy. The creative energy that he had controlled all his life now was turned in on him due to the conscious clutter he allowed his ego to impose on him. Simply put, what had served Solomon reverted back to working against him and became his demons.

42

M A T R I X

How can God be omnipotent and omnipresent? If God is no thing and no thing is pure consciousness, how does God bring God's own thoughts and feelings into physical manifestation? There must be energy of some sort that binds together the elements necessary to create, and this process is guided by mechanisms that are as much scientific as spiritual. God is the original scientist. So, how is it done? In Genesis, God creates light twice. The first light is not of this physical realm. It is the subjective light of God's consciousness. It is the beacon that guides all that is to its highest expression.

Let there be light! This statement reveals much about how God creates. First, it tells us that God is creating light. Second, God doesn't express desire for something that God doesn't have. God doesn't say "I wish" or "Pretty please." God has already defined what it is that God desires, seeing it in its highest state of expression. It is God's subjective view of the desire fulfilled that creates the matrix that binds and guides the evolution of God's desires to their highest expression.

Truly understanding what something is entails knowing both what it is and what it is not. God needs this relative dynamic to define consciousness and everything that comes from it. Bottom line: the first step in creation is knowing what it is that you want to create. Seeing the desire in its state of completion creates the positive charge, while feeling excitement introduces the negative charge to the equation. This interaction of the positive charge with the negative charge causes a vibrational reaction that creates the energy necessary to create and sustain a conscious matrix that attracts the necessary ingredients in the objective realm, allowing that which has been defined to be brought forth into manifestation, where it can be refined. It is the infinite subjective blueprint that creates the matrix that binds and animates this finite objective realm together and creates the matrix that moves the cosmos and is the foundation of creation. The matrix is the defined conscious energy that links the Creator, and that which is to be created, allowing for the interaction necessary for the Creator to be defined through the creation. The created is always defined by the Creator, and it is creation that enables the Creator to be defined.

43

I N T U I T I V E   M A T R I X

At times, the universe seems so abundant with poop that it keeps dropping on us for no apparent reason. Is all this manure the universe's way of telling us it's time for growth? Sometimes that's the case and we should pay attention. We should also know that God is very intuitive and tends to give us what we ask for within the parameters of our personal matrix that brought us into and sustains our Adventure here on earth. Each of our lives has structure that supports who we are and the path we chose at this point in our evolution. Our personal matrix, which was created at the moment of our conception and can be understood using astrology and numerology, works synchronistically with the matrix that was created at the point that we call the "Big Bang" and links each of us with each other and the universe.

As the energy of the matrix moves closer to the perfect defined state of God's wish fulfilled, it supports the universe's, and our, evolution. It is this movement of the energy of the matrix that causes material matter to form and become that which it is, us included. As the matrix moves and expands, what we see as reality unfolds. It is this matrix that supports our Adventure, binds physical matter, and causes the movement of the cosmos in the precise manner that can be observed. This matrix does not rigidly force matter into its assigned expression but rather supports its expression. There is a certain amount of flexibility built into the matrix that allows for the expression of unanticipated interactions of dynamics that might bring forth new expressions into understanding. If creation were limited to what the Creator's understanding was at the point of creation, there would be no evolution of conscious understanding for the Creator, and no new expressions to bring forth new understanding and growth. The intuitive structure that allows for unanticipated interactions of energy, and its effects on this finite realm, allow the observer (us and God) to gain new understanding. The structure that supports the variables that allow for these new unanticipated expressions of the Creative force can be seen and understood within the binary code. This is how a God that knows everything learns new stuff. This flexibility is also built into our connection with each other, God, and All that is.

Our connection to God and each other is intuitive. Have you noticed that even computers have become somewhat intuitive? You start to input information and the computer tries to anticipate what you are inputting before you are finished. Past inputs serve as reference points that enable it to anticipate your requests.

We are continually pushing our computer's keys with our thoughts and feelings, sending out conscious energy that by law must complete the cycle and return to its sender's compatible corresponding energy. If you pay attention, you will notice that sometimes you are generating conscious energy that is not in your best interest and will not return to you something that you want. We all have days when we wake up on the wrong side of the bed with our energy out of balance. If we take the time to go within, be still, and observe what effects the energy is having on us, we can raise our energy up above the negativity before we express it into our lives. Too many times we take our negative conscious energy and dump it onto the people we interact with, giving little thought as to the effects it will have on others and ultimately ourselves. When the poop that you consciously (or unconsciously) requested shows up, you're surprised and upset at the universe for stinking up your day without realizing that it is your thoughts and feelings that brought it about. Once we realize that we are Creators, and that all creation comes from a blending of thought and feeling, we will start paying attention to the thoughts and feelings that we entertain and begin to consciously create a more meaningful life for ourselves and those close to us.

44

Y O U R   M A T R I X

At the very moment of your conception, you are linked to the matrix that supports and sustains creation by your own personal connection that synchronizes you and your energy to this Adventure we see as life as it unfolds. Your free will lies in how you choose to express the supported energy of your personal matrix, bringing it to its highest or lowest expression as you live your life. Each and every aspect of who you are and every possibility that could ever happen in your life is supported by this dynamic. It can be better understood using astrology and numerology. In order for anything to be brought into existence, it must first be defined consciously. But what conscious information is imprinted at that moment of creation? The energy has to know where to go and what to do as your body grows and the person inside gains understanding. We are not plopped down on this earth and left to fend for ourselves. Every moment of our existence is overseen by conscious awareness that supports every aspect of what we call our reality. This conscious energy ranges from very selfless (supporting the big picture) to very personal (supporting your personal Adventure) and everything in between. If not for this synchronistic alignment of All that is, God, we would experience chaos with little meaning and gain little from the experience. The question is, how does it work and how can we take advantage of this energy?

Understand that the conscious energy that is you was set in place at the moment of your conception, and as time unfolds, your physical Adventure marches you towards the perfection that was set in place at that moment. When we move away from the energy that guides our Adventure, we feel the pain as our alignment to our source of power becomes misaligned.

If you take the time to notice, you will note that we always have feelings that constantly swirl and churn inside of us. These feelings respond to the energy that we are entertaining at the moment. When we are in alignment with our matrix, we feel the positive flow of energy and experience the positive effects. Have you ever noticed how good you feel when your focus is on giving to others? This is because you are aligned with the higher vibrational energy of your matrix. You have tapped into energy greater than what is contained within your body (God), giving you added support in your journey into a greater understanding of your limitless abilities. The added joy that comes with this connection to your higher supported energy feels much like having your parents pushing you while on a swing. Instead of having to push and pull yourself to gain momentum, you can relax and feel the force of a power greater than yourself propelling you to ever higher heights, allowing you to gain more enjoyment and growth from the experience. Our true nature is selfless and this is where we feel best consciously.

Our feelings are not static. Some days we feel great; other days, we are challenged with negative energy. The first thing we tend to do is put a face on the energy we are experiencing, fixating on the superficial effects of that energy instead of looking within ourselves to understand how our thoughts and feelings are affecting our lives and the interactions we have with others, moving us a step away from the energy. As we gain understanding of the dynamics of who we are and our relationship to all that is, our lives become more meaningful and consciously productive. We become more attuned to the conscious energy supporting our Adventure and less distracted by the events that manifest from that energy. We start walking a life path that is consciously connected to our defined energy and All that is, God.

We are able to align with our energy, making our lives more meaningful and productive instead of playing catch up trying to rebalance ourselves and our world. Remember that everything is relative. What is must be defined by what it is not. As we cycle through our lives, we experience energy that lifts us up and puts weight on us – we feel good and not good. Without this relative interaction there would be no means of expression. Without pain we would have little understanding of joy. And it is our fear that gives us reference to our courage. Without this relative separation of defined energy, we would have little information to define our reality and our growth would be limited.

The trick is to stay in the moment and pay attention to your feelings, which reveal the truth of the energy you are entertaining here and now. Pain and disease are always experienced up close and personal and can be controlled by shifting your thoughts and feelings from self-centered to selflessly centered. Asking the simple question – how does this serve me? – shifts your perspective from standing in it to standing above it and observing the big picture. This simple shift in consciousness moves you from the realm of the created into the realm of the Creator, where understanding and the wisdom of All that is, God, can be accessed, giving you a stronger conscious connection to energy and wisdom that is greater than yourself. Taking the time and making the effort to understand and work within the supportive energy of your personal matrix will help you to integrate your life into the evolutionary cosmic flow of the matrix that animates creation, seamlessly blending your personal energy with the more impersonal energy of the matrix that animates our universe. This will ultimately bring more meaning and creative understanding into our lives, allowing us to use our free will wisely, working within the energy that supports us and All that is.

This matrix does not define what comes into manifestation but rather is the raw energy available to be defined. Seers who possess the ability to see into the future tap into this matrix and read the energy available at the moment that they wish to view. The reason prophecy is not always spot-on accurate is because the energy supporting any given moment in time and space can be viewed at any time as potential expression, but until it is expressed into manifestation, its defined properties are yet to be established. This is the magic of our free will. Our free will lies in how we choose to express the energy that is available to us and affects how our history unfolds. It is our free will that allows us to bring our role in this Adventure we call life to its highest possible outcome, or something less than perfect, which can raise or lower not only the outcome of our lives, but also have an effect on history in a broader sense. Our lives are scripted with defined energy at the moment of our conception. It is our free choice how we choose to express it.

The planets ride on this matrix, and their precise location can be determined at any time from "Big Bang" until the fulfillment of this Adventure, before returning to pure consciousness (a state of no thingness). Similarly, we can understand where our connection to the matrix will place us using the same wisdom. Astrology reads and helps us to understand the available energy of the matrix at any given point in time and space. It can't tell us what will happen but it can tell us the properties of our aligned energy at any given time.

This connection to the conscious matrix propels our Adventure forward towards the fulfillment of the desired understanding that we came into this particular life to gain. Each of us has a defined agenda into which we were born, and we possess all the ingredients necessary to learn that which we are "destined" to learn. As we move through time and space and experience the energy that allows us to define and refine our conscious energy, it is learning to balance the energy that is available to us that keeps us in the moment, where creation is active, instead of two steps behind trying to bring balance to the imbalances created by our ignorance of our conscious energy. We are supported from the moment of our body's conception until we leave it and return to conscious oneness with God. This support is synchronistically interlocked with the matrix that guides all that is in this physical realm and doesn't adjust to our self-centered needs. It is we who must align and balance with the matrix as the cycle of life progresses, moving us closer to the fulfillment of our defined agenda on our eternal quest to know ourselves and gain enlightenment.

45

THOUGHT AND FEELING

We often hear the words thought and feeling, but do we truly know what the dynamics involved are? Thought and feeling are polar opposites, one being outgoing and the other being receptive. Our thoughts are a formulation of energy generated from within ourselves based on established information we have acquired and are the means by which we articulate and express our feelings and inner consciousness. Thought is outgoing and defines creation. Feelings are the result of the conscious energy we receive and are receptive in nature.

Men think first and their thoughts generate feelings. Women feel first and their feelings generate thoughts. Women are better at remembering words and events because their first inclination is to feel and receive what is being said and done. Men's first inclination is to think, which is outgoing, and their receptivity is secondary to their intellect. While men are busy thinking of what to say next, women are absorbing the information by listening and then instinctively taking mental notes. Ever wonder why women excel at remembering every detail of every discussion they ever had with their husbands? It is this quality that often gives women the upper hand in the conscious dance between the sexes. This doesn't mean that women don't think, it just means their thoughts are formulated after being filtered through their receptive feeling body and have been cataloged within.

Women's ability to hold on to the information gleaned from life and relationships enables them to win more arguments with their significant others, but it also contributes to the fact that women suffer more heart attacks than men as a result of holding onto negative feelings that don't resonate at a healthy vibrational level. Taking the time to think about how their feelings affect them and those they interact with will help in releasing negative feelings that don't serve their highest, most loving expression of self.

Conversely, too many men have marginalized their feelings and instead rely on their intellect to negotiate life without utilizing the intuitive information their feelings give them. A man in touch with his intuitive energy is a more thoughtful individual capable of deeper understanding. Men can use their feelings to balance the energy that supports their thoughts by paying attention to how their thoughts cause them to feel, making adjustments to raise the level in their feeling body.

Women can raise the energy level of their bodies by thinking about their feelings as they are feeling them. The act of analyzing their feelings as they are being experienced enables women to exercise control of their emotions, releasing negative energy that does not feel good or serve their best interest and thus raising their level of conscious expression.

A woman's menstrual cycle exerts effects that go far beyond the physical. This cycle also brings up feelings from deep within, every month on a defined, predictable schedule. Feelings tend to have more depth than intellect making it more difficult to observe the affects they are having on the woman experiencing them and those she interacts with. It is this monthly occurrence that pulls up a woman's deepest feelings, making her more aware of the influence of her intuitive energy on herself and others and allowing her to release emotional energy that does not serve her highest expression of self.

Understanding the dynamics involved in our conscious makeup and the natural flow of thoughts and feelings gives us more control over our lives and ultimately more meaning and fulfillment in our eternal quest to know ourselves, and God.

46

C Y C L E S

Our reality is based on cycles. Creation was started by using cycles, bringing energy from the highest vibrational level to the lowest. Creation is all about getting from Point A, the current state being experienced, to Point B, the desired, defined state envisioned. The matrix that links the Creator, and the desire, to the created expression of that desire, is not linear, it's cyclical, returning to the Creator that which is created. This dynamic can be seen throughout creation from the grand impersonal movement of the cosmos to the cycles that impact our personal lives on a daily basis.

Most of us wake when the sun rises and go to sleep after dark, experiencing this cycle all our lives without looking beyond the obvious dynamics to the creative energy that guides the evolution of the universe and us. With the sunrise, our eyes open, we become conscious, and our egos set out to express and define that conscious energy. We are always connected to God and creation's supportive energy, but while awake, our ego and its outward focus on life's events deflect much of creation's informative energy.

While awake, much of our time is spent generating thoughts, like talking on a walkie-talkie. When our finger is on the button and we are sending conscious information (thoughts), we are not receiving the creative information that truly links us to God and God's creative force. Once the sun goes down and we fall asleep, our ego (conscious mind) lays down and stops transmitting, allowing us to receive guidance from a source greater than ourselves on a nightly basis. All the wisdom we often wake up with comes from this nightly connection with God. If you step back and look from a grander perspective, you will see a daily cycle of consciousness sending and receiving on a global scale as humanity wakes and sleeps, as the earth spins on its 24-hour cycle.

We can understand the energy pushing and pulling on us within our solar system using astrology. These cycles within our solar system, and the universe, connect creation to the creative force (God), guiding the construction of our reality to its ultimate outcome (the perfect expression of consciousness defined). Science can accurately predict the orbits and location of the stars and planets at any point in time and space because of the energy of the matrix that supports physical matter and the defined cycles that support the creative process.

December 21, 2012 was a date that was brought to many people's attention due to the Mayan calendar and the predictions surrounding it. We know it was not the end of the world. What many do not understand is that it was the end of a cycle and the beginning of a new one. The Mayan calendar was based on three calendars woven into one, the first being the Tzolkin calendar, which had a 260-day cycle that may be based on the duration of human pregnancy. The second is the Haab calendar, which is a 365-day solar calendar. The third is the Long Count, which pointed to the end of a cycle on December 21, 2012.

We are now leaving our current cycle, where mankind has been directed by thought, with intuition taking the back seat. We are moving into a new cycle where we will be guided by our intuition grounded in our intellect, a more receptive feminine energy that will foster greater unity and growth on a global scale. This does not mean that women now get their turn riding roughshod over men, but that we will begin to balance the more masculine outgoing energy with a more receptive understanding that will bring us to a true Golden Age of conscious oneness with God and each other.

47

INFINITE ENERGY

What does it mean to be omnipresent and omnipotent? How can God be everywhere and power everything? There has to be dynamics that allows for this, supporting each and every minute detail of creation, guiding everything from light to lead. It has to support everything from big to small, from one's personal Adventure to the unfathomably large movement of the cosmos. Incredibly, the energy that guides this physical experience can be measured precisely, from the very first tick of time through to the very last tick of time.

That force that binds and powers everything is not of this physical realm and can't be measured physically. It's not a matter of seeing smaller; it's a matter of measuring vibrationally finer and lighter. Everything comes from the same source, and its vibrational energy determines its physical properties. The energy that guides and sustains us and the cosmos was set forth in the "Big Bang." In truth, it wasn't an explosion. Explosions blow things apart and are destructive. It was creative in nature, a conscious orgasm, and it bound and defined what we see as our physical reality. Our creation into this world takes place by this simple creative dynamic.

The metaphor of "orgasm" might seem strange, but it's quite apt. An orgasm is creative in nature and is the blending of positive outgoing energy with receptive grounding energy that, when combined, creates a unique vibrational interaction that brings forth energy that is representative of the two combined energies.

Wise men's understanding of infinite conscious energy's effects on the movement of the cosmos has made it possible for them to be aware of special events in our evolution. The birth of Jesus was known to wise men by the alignment of the planets. Nostradamus also used the planets to understand the flow of energy guiding this Adventure we call life. The physical movement of the planets can be measured and predicted. Different alignments create different energy. Knowing this truth allows us to know what energy is available to us at any moment of time because it's very consistent and predictable. This energy is selfless in nature and doesn't bend or waver to any influence. The conscious matrix is created as the final scene in this Adventure, and time and space are marching towards the established conscious conclusion that is already defined by God. Simple examination will support this simple truth.

There is an energy that was set in place at the very moment of creation that guides and supports this Adventure we call life. This energy doesn't tell us what to do; it supports our evolution as conscious beings at the energy level that binds and supports. Stay centered and this energy supports your Adventure at the highest vibrational level. Stray from your cosmic path and your energy wanes, causing discomfort and confusion. Understand that you came with a defined agenda with specific lessons to be learned. Learn to be still and listen to your inner voice (everyone has one) and your Adventure will bear fruit.

48

THE ALIGNMENT OF THE PLANETS AND EVOLUTION

There is nobody like you; you are truly unique. But what is it that gives each of us our own unique characteristics? We tend to take our reality for granted without looking beyond the superficial or realizing that everything from lead to light had to be created, defined, and synchronistically put into play to allow for what we see as reality to unfold.

We are eternal conscious beings experiencing this finite world in our eternal quest for discovery as children of God. While you are the person you see in the mirror, you are far greater than what you and others perceive. Remember you are eternal, conscious in nature, and transcend time and space. Simply put, you existed before you were you, and you will continue to be after you are finished being who you are. Your infinite eternal identity is consciously connected to All that is (God) and has access to all knowledge, which does not allow for the self-centered sense of separation we experience here on earth. In Heaven you are limited to the all-knowing wisdom of the Creator, lacking the ability to see yourself as being separate from God and All that is. Your lives lived in physical form as a finite being allow you to gain wisdom that comes from a perspective 180 degrees from the selfless eternal state you come from and will return to. The vehicle you see as being you was created as a means of expression with defined properties that allow you to express yourself in your unique manner.

So, how does it work? First off, your body is the result of evolution – a blending of specific energy that is transferred from generation to generation, continually adding and blending energy that defines your genetic makeup. The Biblical phrase, "The sins of the father are passed onto the son" describes this genetic dynamic.

Our bloodline, or family tree, gives us specific genetic energy. How that energy gets expressed is determined by the time and place of our conception, fine-tuned by the time and place of our birth. At the time of what science calls the "Big Bang," the very first thing that came into being was the matrix that defines this physical realm. In the Bible, God created light twice. The second light is what illuminates and can be seen in this finite world. The first light that was created has energy that vibrates at a rate that can't be detected in this finite physical realm. It is that light that physical matter is attracted to, sustained by, and rides upon.

The moment in time and space that you were born gives you your unique connection to the matrix, which itself provides you your unique way of expressing your genetic energy. Your genetic energy is unique to you as is your alignment to the matrix. At the moment of your conception, the genetic information from your mother and father was joined, giving you your unique genetic makeup which was linked to the matrix that supports creation and the movement of the cosmos. Each moment in time and space has a unique alignment that supports creation.

This energy is constantly moving and is what animates the movement of everything within the physical universe, you included. Your alignment to this energy (the matrix) is unique to you as it is for all living beings. Identical twins born within moments of each other will have their own unique connection into the matrix, giving them their own special identity within their apparent similarities. The brilliance of the matrix is that everyone has their own alignment, making everyone unique, giving each individual a life path that serves their growth at this point in their evolution as eternal children of God. As the matrix moves, so do the cosmos, and your alignment to the matrix is also continually shifting, empowering you to move forward and express a new and improved you, each and every moment of your life.

49

THE FULCRUM

We come from a selfless perspective before making the leap into self-centered expression, only to have to struggle back to where we came from. What's the point? What do we get for our efforts? Power, and the ability to create consciously. Remember, we are created in God's image and are growing into our potential.

The energy that powers our Adventure is relative. Light requires dark to define it, up needs down in order to define its nature. You can't define good unless you have something to define it – bad. We tend to judge the events of our lives without taking into account the dynamics of this relative law. It is the bad days that help to define the good days, our sad moments that give a reference point to our moments of joy, and our pain that defines our pleasure. Without these relative separations, our existence would be rather bland and far less meaningful. We come from a state of conscious oneness with God. The Fall is the conscious shift from We to Me. As we gain our sense of self (our I am), we establish a conscious point of reference (our I am) that is 180 degrees from the state we come from, oneness with God.

Our connection with God is never broken and never can be. We are God and God is greater. Think of oneness with God as being held close by your parents: nuzzled into their warmth, you can't see anything because you're wrapped in their loving arms, and your view is obscured. You feel the affection and warmth but can't see anything. The Fall is your parents setting you down so you can experience all the possibilities that this Adventure offers. It's a new sensation and a bit frightening, but your parents are right behind you, supporting your every move. All you need to do is remember to turn around from time to time (go within) to see they haven't left.

How do we do that? Be still and know I am. Our connection to God is conscious and we maintain our connection by taking time to still our minds and listen to the silence. It is within the silence of our hearts and minds that we find the guidance that brings true meaning to this Adventure, guidance that is always correct.

As we learn to shift our focus from the physical world and go within to the conscious realm of creation, we develop a point of balance. At first, most of the weight is on the physical so our focus leans that way, but as we learn to go within, our point of balance begins to shift from the created towards the creative side of life. We begin to create rather than react. We step into a partnership with God, actively involved in creating a prosperous Adventure for ourselves and those we touch.

When balancing on a fulcrum, our focus has to be in the moment to stay on top. If we focus on what's behind us, we tend to fall on our rump. If we focus and fret on the future, we are likely to fall on our face, and even if we don't quite fall, we aren't balanced and in control of our Adventure. Understand that there are variables in the equation we call life. These variables are what imbues our Adventure with meaning. While your personal matrix was set in place at the moment of your conception, with every possible event written into the energy that is you, your free will gives you the ability to bring your Adventure to its highest or lowest expression. That's the brilliance that this Adventure offers us: the ability to express, define, and refine who we are while being completely supported by All that is.

Learning to stay in the moment, listening to the vibrational information that comes from within and allowing us to express a balanced expression of self-centered and selflessly centered conscious energy gives us wisdom. With this wisdom, we can enjoy the passion of being in it while having access to the knowledge that comes from rising above it. Being balanced requires effort, but the changes that come with living in the moment and balancing our thoughts and feelings are well worth it.

50

WHAT IS REAL AND WHAT IS NOT?

What is real and what is not? The question is deceptively simple, but there is more than meets the eye (quite literally). For example, we often think something is real because the five senses say it's so. That's our reality. We see our home as real. Will it stand forever? No. We see our favorite shirt as real, but at what point does it get old and tattered and become a rag? We see money as real, but can't it be taken from us at any moment with little or no notice? What do we take with us when we leave this life?

Why do we invest so much energy into acquiring stuff that is just going to rust, tear, and turn to dust? Though we need stuff to conduct our lives in the manner that we see fit, we become so caught up in stuff that we have forgotten its true purpose, a means by which we can express, define, and refine ourselves to our highest expression. That is the purpose for this physical realm. So, should we not have stuff? No, all the great stuff in this world is here for us to use as a means to express ourselves, define that expression, and then refine that definition to its highest level, taking theory and putting it into practice, seeing what works and what does not and making adjustments. The trick is remembering what we get to keep and what gets left behind.

We are here to gain understanding and add to our conscious identity as eternal children of God, adding layer upon layer of conscious information and giving us more depth as individuals. Not all the experience we gain serves our highest expression of who we are, and some aspects must be eliminated from our conscious identity to get to our most refined expression of self, much like chipping away the excess marble that obscures the perfect form within. You are in many ways like the block of marble that Michelangelo turned into the statue of David.

It has been told that for some time, Michelangelo had the block of marble that became David. He looked at that block of marble until he began to see the potential within, and then he started patiently chipping away at what was not the most perfect expression of that block of marble. Sometimes his view of perfection was spot on, and he could chip away with ease and clarity, while at other times in the process the vision of perfection became clouded and unclear. It was during these times of doubt, as frustrating as they were, that the artist (Creator) had to exercise patience, stop the rush forward, step back, and seek guidance from within. This is done by being still, posing the question, and going within, knowing the answer is coming.

Pay attention: God speaks to us with our thoughts and feelings. God inspires us with the events of our lives; there are no coincidences. Everything that comes into our lives has purpose; everyone you meet has something for you. The people and stuff that we have in our lives are here to allow us to express, define, and refine ourselves. We are already perfect. The events of our lives give us more substance to add to our perfect sense of self. Going within allows us to chip away at what obscures that perfection.

Use the things in your life to express and define yourself, but remember that they are here for that purpose, so don't lose yourself in things that rust, tatter, and rot away. What we take with us is our conscious understanding, not the things we accumulate. Remember why you are here: to gain self-awareness, and to refine that awareness to its highest expression, allowing you to gain remembrance of your selfless relationship with All that is (God).

Remember that God and you are one and God is greater. By refining yourself (chipping away at the marble that obscures the perfection of the David), you free that perfect child of God that is you. There are no words that can express the joy that this selfless awareness brings into your life. Your clarity of self allows you to be one with God and live in a state of love, light, and transcendent bliss.

51

T R U T H   I S   S E L F - E V I D E N T

An ongoing debate continues around the question of evolution vs. creation, but what is often overlooked is the question of the structure supporting reality itself. A structure that would support creation at its humble beginnings and allow for expression and expansion of greater and more complex energy. It appears that evolution is a mindless continuum of fortunate coincidences which, if you do the math, doesn't add up. On the other hand, religions' view of a grey-haired old man spending six days to whip up All that is will, on close inspection, lead one to the same conclusion. It too will not add up. There is a great deal of information written into the Genesis story, but the self-evident truth has been obscured by the story itself, and simple logic must be used to understand the creative process that brought this physical realm into existence.

"Truth is self-evident," a fundamental notion that both science and religion should agree upon. Our reality is based on established truths. These truths support the big picture and if you know how to look, you can see it even in the biggest lie. The truth about the nature of reality has, from the very first tick of conscious energy, always presented itself. This simple truth was established and became self-evident when God's attention turned in on itself and God realized I am. The complexity we see as our reality is the result of countless expressions of infinite conscious energy being brought in and out of finite existence, where the self-evident results of each creative expression have led to the next. Evolution has, from the very beginning, been consciously guided by the self-evident truth that comes with creation.

52

T R E E

One glance at a tree will demonstrate that the taller the tree, the deeper the roots. You will also notice that the tree receives most of its nourishment through the roots closest to the surface and its structural support from the deepest roots. Just like us, a tree is brought into the physical realm via the intermingling of masculine and feminine energy and grows from seed to maturity guided by a predetermined matrix. The tree also grows toward the light and, just like us, the essential purpose of the tree is to allow conscious energy to be expressed and refined, evolving from generation to generation.

There are certain characteristics that we share with trees. Like a tree, growing closer to the light requires deeper roots. As the part of the tree that can be seen represents your life, the part that can't be seen represents the support we receive in this physical realm that comes from within (God). The taller a tree grows, the more support is required to keep it upright and growing toward the light. A tree lacking a deep, well-developed root system is easily toppled in a harsh environment. Do you see this truth within us?

A person who invests their energy into superficial distractions at the expense of inner growth (knowing oneself) will lack the inner wisdom (roots) to remain anchored during turbulent times. The quiet time we spend knocking on the conscious door of Heaven, going within, asking the questions that burn in our hearts like young excited children knowing their more knowledgeable parents have the answers, is our path to deep roots and a strong conscious bond to Heaven and All that is.

The events and interactions of our lives represent the roots closest to the surface. It is these events and interactions that give us the relative experiences that can raise our conscious energy, strengthening our rooted connection to God and our true creative force, or weaken us consciously and lower our creative energy. What we choose to do within the structure of our daily lives brings us the opportunities to define and nourish us, and brings us closer or moves us further from our truth, and God. Life is about growth, and it is our conscious growth that we take with us when we leave this life.

For a tree to grow strong, it needs water. Like a tree, we need nourishment to grow both our body and the soul within. What we do with our interactions with people and the events of our lives nourishes the soul, while maintaining our inner connection to God keeps the natural flow of sustenance flowing like water.

The thing you see in the mirror is your temple, a vehicle allowing you, the eternal being within, to experience this relative world. If your attention is on the physical, you're a few steps behind creation, with less creative support. When you are consciously aware, in the moment where everything is created, you can create within the structure of the moment as it unfolds, utilizing energies and wisdom greater than yourself and strengthening your connection to your higher creative energy. This is much more graceful than having to attempt to rebalance the results of ignorant actions as they unfold.

53

THE MEAL

Why do we poop? A world where nothing poops surely would be much nicer. There would probably be no flies to pester us. And then there is the stink! Could it be that God just couldn't come up with a better design? Or could it be that we, and all living things, are created according to the law of creation, and, understanding the truth of that law, are designed to allow God to express, define, and refine in the most effective way?

Think about the process. First, there is hunger, which in simple terms is an emptiness needing to be fulfilled. If you fill it with something that is nourishing, your body gets the most nourishment it can get and has to do the least amount of work to process the nourishment from the part that is not useful to the body. You get more nourishment than poop. Alternatively, you can choose something that will gratify your senses but has little or no nutritional value. Your body has to work harder to process all the stuff that doesn't nourish you and gets little or nothing for its trouble. You get lots of poop and little nourishment.

If you look at the process of the body and what happens in your body from the point you feel hunger to the point where you poop, you will be amazed to find that the archetypal structure of creation is, in effect, supporting and evolving everything, both the infinite consciousness of the Creator and the finite created manifestation, our bodies included, using the same eternal law. Life is like a meal. We can choose to focus our conscious energy (thoughts and feelings) on a positive level, raising ourselves and those we interact with up into a more joyful, meaningful experience. Or, we can choose to be negative and lower our conscious energy, affecting ourselves and everyone around us. The quality of our lives depends on the choices we make, much like the health of our bodies is dependent on how we feed and care for them.

Remember that what you perceive as reality is an expression of consciousness, designed from God's conscious understanding of creation based on countless adventures into the creative realm of consciousness. God has had a lot of time to figure out the most effective means of expressing, defining, and refining what's possible, and that's what God and we are all about. Think about it. Everything from movement to what we see as physical stuff is an expression being defined and hopefully refined. What we perceive as real is a projection of consciousness and has a fundamental structure running through it from the highest vibrational levels of creation to the lowest vibrational levels of created matter. Understanding this simple truth on the infinite conscious level of creation allows us to negotiate the created physical realm with power and purpose.

God, being all that there is, has to not only create everything but define it and bring it to its highest expression (refine it). Remember that all this comes from no thing (pure consciousness). God can't simply order out, so there is a-lot going on. Everything has to work synchronistically. Energy has to be available to fuel growth (evolution), and there can't be any parts left over. There are more than a couple laws and principles involved in creation. One of those laws is the relative law of separation. Separating consciousness into thought and feeling, separating light from dark, in from out, and up from down. Separation is necessary to define what is from what it is not. Understand that it is what something is not that helps define what it is, and once you have that which is defined, you have to do something with the leftovers or else there's going to be a whole lot of mess cluttering up the place.

God has to figure out what to do with all this leftover stuff that was the byproduct of creation. Remember, God is all there is and has to do everything in house. God can't put the trash out on Tuesday and expect it to be gone on Wednesday – where would it go? God had to figure out how to get rid of all the extra stuff that didn't serve the highest expression of God's focus. There had to be a means to utilize this excess stuff, leaving no thing. There needed to be a practical use for poop that not only disposed of it but utilized it, in a way that would benefit the ceaseless evolutionary progression of existence.

Living in the moment and being aware of the energy you entertain and express raises your conscious energy to a level that creates more meaningful interactions, yielding more nourishment than poop. In essence, the story of Job was all about poop and how it fueled his evolution from a self-centered righteous man into a selfless righteous man. The poop that Job had to deal with stank and drew flies, but he ultimately grew into a selfless man who was able to walk this earth consciously one with God, and that is why we are here.

There is truth in everything. Separating truth from what is not truth is what nourishes God and us, God's children. If you have trouble understanding the truth about something, look to what it is not and start removing the aspects that don't support the truth. The poop that shows up in our lives has a purpose. Use it wisely and your growth will bloom like a well-fed garden. Stomping and sloshing in it will only track stink everywhere and draw flies.

54

FAITH

What is faith? Is it what you have while you are waiting for something better or waiting for the suffering to stop? Is it permission to coast through life ignorant and with a minimum of effort, or could it be the energy that creates, attracts, and maintains everything that is, pure subjective awareness focused on creation in its perfect state of fulfillment (completion).

Faith is pure subjective energy vibrating at a rate of perfect fulfillment. When conscious awareness is focused upon a desired state of being and that desired state is held in a perfect unwavering subjective state of fulfillment, the vibrational energy created by the focused view of the wish fulfilled creates a vibrational void in the matrix that must be filled. It is God's law of creation.

The feeling of the wish fulfilled is the negative side of the creative force that brings forth conscious energy into this physical objective realm of expression. When the vibrational energy of the wish fulfilled (feeling) is unwaveringly wrapped around the thought of the wish (the desired state of being perfectly expressed), the vibrational energy created by the joy (negative plus positive) intermingles with the positive energy of the wish and bursts forth into the physical objective realm as pure energy. This energy provides the matrix that brings forth and maintains all the necessary ingredients to bring pure consciousness (thought and feeling) into physical reality.

In Genesis, the first time God said let there be light, it was not light like from the sun; it was lighter than light. This light vibrates at a higher, finer rate. Think of pure subjective thought as the highest level of vibration. Lower the vibrational pulse a little and you get the matrix that supports all physical matter, from light to lead. What we see as physical light vibrates at a lower rate than the matrix. While light vibrates within the physical realm of expression, the matrix vibrates above the vibrational level of this physical realm and therefore cannot be measured as physical matter. Science is calling it dark energy.

The best way to measure the matrix is to measure its effect on physical matter. While it vibrates within the subjective non-physical realm of existence, it supports everything in the physical, objective realm of expression. It is our faith that enables us to interact with the matrix, influencing our Adventure by directing the energy that supports it. Again, this is done by subjectively envisioning the desired state of being in its perfect state of expression and maintaining an unwavering view of that perfect expression.

It is faith, not gravity, that causes the planets to move in perfect synchronicity. It is faith that attracts, binds, and maintains every aspect of existence without exception, moving the planets on their appointed paths, allowing God's (our) awareness to stretch and expand on God's (our) never-ending journey of self-discovery. After all, everything that is, from top to bottom, beginning to end, is about God (God and we are one and God is greater) expressing, defining, and refining God. It is God's faith that perfectly supports God's journey of discovery, allowing God (us) to experience God (ourselves).

55

THE VEIL

How would you define pure? In our pre-Fall state of innocence, we were pure, having nothing to define us other than God. Think of it as a clear glass of water. Our Fall was like flavor being added to the water. At first the flavor is diluted by the water so that only a hint of taste is present; the liquid remains clear, and it is still called water. Every experience we have in our lifetime adds flavor to our glass, and each person's experience has unique flavor.

The water is who we truly are, God. The flavor is our I am and the water is our omnipresent, omnipotent connection to All that is, God. As the events of our lives add to this flavor of who we are, our I am becomes stronger and more defined as we experience life's events.

We are conscious beings. Our power lies within our consciousness, and it is our thoughts and feelings that inform us as to the vibrational correctness of that which we entertain. Thoughts and the actions that come from our conscious minds create vibrational energy that constantly inform us as to the level of conscious energy we are entertaining. Self-centered focus adds flavor to your consciousness while creating more separation from your true self, God.

Shifting your focus from your self-centered perspective and asking the question "How does this serve me?" moves your conscious focus from the Me side of the equation to the We side, allowing you to observe your energy and how the thoughts and feelings you entertain affect you on a conscious energy level. This process allows you to exercise aspects of who you are that don't support your highest expression of self, clarifying your glass of water and allowing you to walk the face of this wonderful earth consciously connected to All that is, God. We keep all the experience we gain on our Adventures, but now we have access to the wisdom of God.

The process of observation of our inner thoughts and feelings allows us to remove the veil of ego that obscures the truth of who we are and reconnects us to All the authentic power that we possess as children of God, leaving us consciously connected to God, and All that is. This is what Jesus and all great masters do, a truth that resonates in the statement, "The things I do, you will do, and greater."

As we balance our conscious energy back towards the We side of the equation life becomes more meaningful. We begin to perceive things beyond the limitations of our five senses, enriching our lives with greater meaning. We begin to understand things we always have felt on a deep level but were unable to pull up into our conscious minds because of the obstructive flavor. The process of observing our thoughts and the feelings that they create returns our glass of water to a clear state of purity and allows us to gain access to God and All of God's wisdom.

56

E M P T Y   &   F U L L

We live in a state of relative consciousness. We understand light because of the dark that gives definition to it. We know up because of down, in because of out. If we pay attention, we can see this separation of qualities defining everything.

Fullness is the state of being in which we dwelled in the state of innocence in the Garden of Eden. We were full of love, but we could not see it in all its glory because that's all there was. Its all-consuming totality made it so that we had nothing to help us define it. We knew God's light but could not see its beauty because all there was was light. We had nothing to distinguish it from and thus nothing to define it. Though it was frightening, our Fall into the emptiness of this objective realm is what bestowed on us the ability to see what we have in all its Glory. It is emptiness that gives us the room and desire to fill ourselves with the ingredients necessary to help us grow in our eternal quest for self-realization. We can see the powerful beauty of the relationship between emptiness and fullness in our physical bodies every day.

As we wake up hungry (empty), we decide what to consume to rid ourselves of that emptiness; our bodies then take it and digest it, utilizing what nourishes us to support us and our growth. That which does not nourish us is eliminated, leaving us empty, which gives our bodies more room to add more nourishment, allowing for more growth. Our bodies are continually moving from a state of emptiness to a state of fullness and back again.

We tend to focus on our state of fullness, choosing not to see the purpose and the beauty of the state of emptiness. For most of us, emptiness is an unpleasant state of being that is to be avoided or cured as quickly as possible, without much thought as to its purpose in our evolutionary journey of self-realization. If we were always full, we would have no need or desire to be fulfilled, and where would we put fulfillment with no empty space to put it?

The state of emptiness is often uncomfortable. If it were not uncomfortable we would not feel compelled to fill it. We would not seek nourishment with the same enthusiasm we do now. It is our desire to fill the void which moves us forward in our eternal quest for self-realization. Getting past the fear that surrounds our emptiness is what prevents us from embracing our emptiness and using it to our advantage.

How we can move past the fear is to start questioning what empty feels like. Fear is always supported by ignorance, and looking beyond our fear into what we feel as our emptiness raises our focus up above the emptiness, where we can understand the driving force behind that emptiness. What does our emptiness do to our physical bodies? How does it make us feel mentally and emotionally? By asking ourselves these questions, we open up a dialogue with that All-knowing part of us that is God. By looking and questioning with an open heart and mind, we gain access to wisdom that is All-knowing. As we pay attention to our thoughts and feelings, we see the most perfect path to take to fulfillment of our desires. As we begin to see our emptiness as the powerful blessing that it is, we can use it to gain a true sense of fulfillment, accelerating our self-realization.

This brilliant, loving energy that is God envelops us wholly. There is no place that we can go physically, mentally, emotionally or spiritually, where God is not there supporting our every thought, feeling, and action. When we feel empty, and the uncertainty that goes with it, know that God is right here, right now, to fill us with the best, brightest possible expression of self that we can imagine. Knowing this will bring new meaning to our emptiness, giving us a sense of security that enables us to boldly go where no mere mortal could ever go and to fill ourselves with all the greatness that we are. Understanding that it was a void (emptiness) within God that pulled God's selfless awareness in on itself, starting this great Adventure, and that it is emptiness that always precedes and makes space for creation, bringing new meaning and purpose to our emptiness.

57

If you want to grow stronger physically, you know to pick up weight and start moving. The added weight plus forward movement burns fat (fuel) and develops strength, disposing of that which doesn't serve the body (fat). You want to grow stronger intellectually, you know to take on the burden of study. The act of taking in new information causes the brain to formulate new concepts, needing specific information to support this new information.

In the process, preexisting concepts that run contrary to new knowledge and understanding have to be reconciled. This relative exercise can be quite exhausting but will ultimately yield a clearer, grander understanding. Quite often the truth is already within our realm of understanding but has been obscured by inaccurate beliefs. Call this the fat of the mind. It serves nothing but your ignorance of the truth and adds useless conscious weight to your intellect.

Emotional growth can be painful because it typically entails more destruction than construction. Deep within us, we are already perfect. The fat of our emotional bodies hides this truth, and as we begin to exercise and this untruth is burned away, we get a glimpse at our truth. This energizes us, making it easier to work harder.

As we exercise our intellect, we burn off old outdated concepts that don't serve our new understanding. We can put this new understanding to work right away, helping us to negotiate life with more power and meaning. Though it's taxing for the brain and for our intellect, the net gain is positive.

We can embrace negative emotions for so long that they become familiar; they may even become a part of us, or our identity. This familiarity is very personal and we tend to hold our emotions very close to us consciously. Sometimes they are so close as to induce short-sightedness; once again, we can't see beyond, we can't see the forest for the trees. We need separation and distance to be able to see clearly. We need to get above our emotions so we can monitor them with clarity.

Pain of any kind is personal and is experienced up close as part of us. As we separate consciously from that which we focus upon, our view broadens. Much like standing in the middle of a crowd, you hear and feel all the commotion, but your perspective is blocked by the close proximity of those around you. Now, step into the basket of a balloon and rise above the crowd, and suddenly your perspective changes. As you hover over the crowd, you can see more clearly. The higher you go, the more selfless your view becomes. Now that you have a better view of the big picture, you can lower your conscious mind back down to the ground (your personal perspective) and navigate the moment that is your life more effectively.

However, there is a paradox at work here: the same thing (being "among the crowd") that limits our perspective simultaneously broadens it. This is what separates us from mere angels. While Angels are limited to the view of the big picture (up in the balloon), our Fall has given us the ability to stand in it and have that very personal perspective that standing in it affords us. What made Jesus unique was that he returned to the selfless understanding of God and the Angels, being born again into the view from Heaven, the big picture. This knowledge and the strength that exercising aspects of self that didn't serve that understanding gave Jesus the ability to travel consciously, anywhere he chose, from Heaven to Hell and everywhere in between at will. This is what being a child of God is all about: total freedom to stand and create with God. While given to us as our birthright, we must grow and mature in order to wield this power wisely. After all, we are talking about creation.

Physical, intellectual, emotional, and spiritual growth all come from exercise. We are not static but in fact are always growing stronger or weaker. Impose a burden on someone. If they move that burden, they grow stronger. If they choose not to, they live with the weight and grow weaker as the burden limits movement and atrophies their strength. We are here to grow.

58

T H E   I L L U S I O N

For most people, reality is based on the perspective of the created, seeing ourselves as physical beings, separate from each other and God. God is seen as a physical being, very much separate from us. Heaven and Hell are physical locations separate from us in an undisclosed distant part of the universe. God loves us but is really pissed about something Adam and Eve did way back when. We were yet to be born, but God is still angry. And then there's the devil. We can't decide if the devil is locked in a life and death struggle with God for his very existence or if the devil is just out to get us. Either way, it sounds pretty scary.

Our fear comes from our ignorance of the truth. Once we realize that we truly are eternal conscious beings that lived prior to this life and will continue to exist once we leave our physical, finite bodies, the veil of the illusion many of us are under will be lifted, bringing new meaning to our lives. We will begin to realize that the Kingdom of God (Heaven) is, and always has been, right under our noses, cleverly hidden within each and every one of us.

Heaven is not a physical place. It is a state of consciousness and is always right here, right now. We just have to remember to be still and turn our attention 180 degrees and look inward. Once we remember this simple method of connecting with God and all that is, the illusion begins to take on new meaning as a true means of expressing and defining who we truly are and refining our conscious awareness to its highest expression. With this simple knowledge, we begin to see the natural flow of conscious energy that empowers and guides our Adventure. We begin to ride this unique energy that is always available to us, much like riding a wave instead of swimming against it. We begin to see the challenges that life brings us as an opportunity for growth instead of dreaded moments of pain and struggle. What once was unbearable and frightening becomes manageable and meaningful. This simple change in perspective will benefit you wondrously. Pay attention!

59

L I F E   A N D   D E A T H

What idiot thought up death? Who is to blame? You can blame life for death. You can also thank death for life, for we exist in a relative world. If there were no death, how would you perceive life? What value could you put on life?

What imbues life with its grand value is the fact that we view it as something that can be taken from us at any moment for no apparent reason. Yet what is its purpose? This physical realm with its relative polarities allows us to bring ideas, concepts, and the emotions attached to them into being so that they can be expressed, defined, and refined. This allows us to grow and gain an understanding of self that would not be possible without a physical, relative environment to express, define, and refine them in.

Everyone wants to be immortal! What would it be like to live forever? Sounds great, but think about the most perfect day of your life; imagine the joy you felt, and how you wish it could last forever. Disneyland is a blast. Day one, you're in Heaven and you never want to leave. Day ten, you know it like the back of your hand. You're still having fun, but the thrill has already waned. Now imagine Disneyland after an eternity.

At what point does Heaven (Disneyland) start feeling like Hell? We and God are eternal beings. Our ability to die (leave our state of consciousness) and be born again into a yet higher state of consciousness, without having to pack all the baggage from our last trip (life), allows us to travel light and maneuver through each Adventure without the added burden of excess karma (baggage), hindering our Adventure.

Our ability to pick a life that will support our growth in a specialized manner allows each and every one of us to gain our own unique sense of self that gives the creative force (God) a wealth of omnipresent, omnipotent awareness. Having the ability to gain defined understanding in a given lifetime, leave that life, and continually reincarnate into new lives that support ever-growing and diverse understanding allows for efficient and rapid evolution as eternal beings.

To say that eternity is a really long time is a huge understatement. Look at the time we spend on this earth in one lifetime and compare that to the life span of the universe, and then realize that there have been countless "Big Bangs" and will be countless more, and you will get a small glimpse of the big picture. Our ability to come and go in and out of this finite world experiencing many unique lives supports our eternal growth and brings meaning and joy to our journey of self-discovery. Growth is what fuels and brings meaning to God's and our existence, and without the ability to step from lifetime to lifetime, our existence would be far less meaningful and downright boring.

Life is made precious because of the existence of what we call death. A wise person understands this and loves everyone with all their heart, every moment of their life, knowing that this is a temporary state that should be valued for all it is worth. Death releases us from this portion of our journey so we can progress into new learning environments on our eternal journey of evolution into ever-higher expressions of perfection.

60

S T R U G G L E

Life is a struggle that begins with the trauma of birth. Both newborn and mother struggle as the child emerges into the world: both the created and the Creator struggle. There is no free lunch, and creation requires that energy be invested into the process. What binds the created to the Creator is energy. This energy is also what binds us to God consciously, binds our physical finite bodies to our infinite conscious selves, and binds us, and All that is, together.

Reality is a synchronized dance between Creator and created; consciously linked energy being expressed on a myriad of levels as it sustains reality. What we are aware of is only a very small portion of the energy involved. This energy binds every molecule in your body and all of the substance of the finite realm, allowing matter to form and express all its unique properties, from light to lead. This energy is infinite, transcends time and space, empowers and records all expressions in this finite, physical realm, and is what remains in eternity after the finite expression ceases to exist. Our ignorance of this natural flow of energy contributes to the suffering that we experience.

We are always growing; we never stop. Life is not static. We can become knowledgeable and open-minded, or small-minded and opinionated. We can become stronger or weaker, fit or fat. It's all relative and depends on what we choose. Growth requires an investment of energy and that often involves a struggle of some kind. If we invest our energy wisely, the struggle yields the best results; conversely, mindless behavior produces a struggle that yields only suffering, with little positive growth. What we are meant to receive from our mistakes is wisdom if we pay attention. Otherwise, our mistakes become habits that inhibit our progress. We truly are created in God's conscious image and just like God, we are all about gaining wisdom and the conscious strength that comes with our growth.

61

SUFFERING

Suffering is not only pain. Suffering is also about growth. People tend to be so overwhelmed by suffering that quite often they miss the blessings in disguise, hidden amidst the pain. When you exercise your body, you feel discomfort. The result of your pain and suffering is a stronger, fitter body. When you go to school to learn, you may struggle with the mental effort involved in acquiring new knowledge. Yet the benefit of your suffering is more understanding. You become more capable and intellectually you have grown. When you fall in love and experience the joy and pain that comes with being in love, the joy of being together lifts your soul and the pain of separation feels like a knife in your heart. Losing love can be indescribably miserable, but if we choose to grow from our suffering, we become wiser, stronger, and better as a result. We gain understanding that make us more sensitive to the feelings of others and we become better lovers.

Sometimes, we find ourselves lost, spiritually lost. Sometimes something happens to cause us to fall into darkness; sometimes we seem to just wake up in it. These moments of trial and tribulation drain our happiness, health, peace of mind, and faith. You find yourself empty and devoid of hope. It really sucks.

You can suffer for days, weeks, months, or years. Spiritual suffering can be very painful because of the depth of our souls. Sometimes the pain is so deep within us that we can't find a way to get to it. Every time we try, the pain increases or our soul seems to crawl deeper into the darkness, making it difficult to see the problem, let alone understand it.

Sometimes you are so overwhelmed that all you can do is hide from yourself. Some pain seems so great that nothing and no one can alleviate it. No doctor or drug can seem to make it go away. This is a moment in our life when we need to go within and start talking to God and ourselves (it is all the same). Find a quiet spot whenever possible, be still, and talk to God. Express your feelings concerning the challenge that faces you like you were talking to the wisest, most loving being you could imagine, because you are. You already have the perfect answer to every challenge you could ever have; know this.

Having expressed your concerns and desires, know that God (All that is) has set forth the light (matrix) that will attract all the necessary ingredients for the realization of your deepest desires. We are in a partnership with God, and God knows our pain and knows that being wounded opens us up to rapid growth. Let God do the heavy lifting. God is really good at it and loves helping. Once we allow God to assist us with our suffering, a lightness comes over us and our environment, lifting us, our spirit, and our physical circumstances. Pay attention to your thoughts and feelings that accompany them; that is how God directs you. Your suffering will make you stronger, gentler, wiser, more humble, more open, and more loving. So, suffer unto God.

62

F E A R

What is fear and what is its purpose? Fear is a natural evolution of the conscious energy of the Beast. Imagine the first act of aggression: gerbil #1 decides for the very first time that he wants what gerbil #2 has. But gerbil #2 isn't sharing. Gerbil #1 moves in and gives a nudge; gerbil #2 nudges back. Back and forth the energy of their selfish desire is exercised, growing stronger and more defined with each exchange until it bursts forth into this physical realm in the form of a back fist to the face of gerbil #2.

At the point that fist meets face, there are two exchanges of energy: the physical meeting of two opposing forces, fist and face, and the exchange of the energy animating the physical act. Gerbil #1 experiences the aggressive, outgoing side of fear – I want it, I'm taking it. This side of fear pulls all of the attention inward – I want it, I need it, I'm going to have it. The anticipation of the upcoming act of aggression gets the blood pumping and ready to support the body in its act of aggression, bringing all the senses to a state of extreme alertness. Gerbil #2 feels the physical impact of gerbil #1's fist on his face. The impact sends shockwaves through his body. The lungs gasp for oxygen and the heart starts pounding, pushing the blood to feed the body and adrenaline to speed up reactions to aid in self-preservation. All awareness is brought to focus on the moment, all senses are heightened, ready for fight or flight.

Fear in its true form is designed for one purpose — survival. It heightens awareness and feeds the body, acutely boosting its speed, power, and agility. Once the danger is over, we are designed to return to our natural state of calm, focused awareness.

Living in a state of fear creates a state of unease, or "dis-ease." When we are in a state of fear-based thinking, our body's vibration is off balance. This imbalance is what we feel as dis-ease. If this energy is allowed to continue being expressed in an unbalanced manner for a prolonged time, the dis-ease begins to settle into the body as a physical ailment (disease). Think of an engine with one spark plug wire disconnected. When you run your engine, you feel the imbalance, put stress on your engine, and the imbalance becomes more pronounced, but the car still runs and you can still run errands. If you take the time to diagnose the problem and correct the imbalance, no permanent damage is incurred. If the imbalance is allowed to go unchecked, it can wear down other parts of the body physically and the energy that animates it.

Dis-ease is always caused by negative energy-causing discordant vibrations in the energy field that animates our bodies. Dis-ease settles into the physical body from the energy that animates it. The fastest way to cure a disease is to balance the discordant energy that animates it. For example, smoking is a common cause of lung cancer. It's the physical smoke being inhaled into the lungs that causes the disease; science has proven that. But if disease were purely physical, science should be able to determine that you get lung cancer after smoking cigarette number 34,585, give or take a cigarette or two. Why do some people smoke all their lives and never get cancer while some people get it after smoking 10 or 15 years, and still others get cancer even though they have never smoked? Science can't explain away all these variables by looking only at the physical body. It is our energy and its interaction with this physical realm that defines and maintains our three-dimensional reality.

The kingdom of Heaven that Christ spoke of is this realm of pure energy. How our energy (the real us) interacts with our bodies (the vehicle that allows us to express, define, and refine our true nature) is what determines our physical state of being and the three-dimensional reality that surrounds it. If we allow our conscious energy to vibrate at the lower levels of fear-based expression, it will affect us on all levels: our spiritual bodies, our emotional and mental states, and our physical bodies. Taking the time and effort to monitor and elevate our conscious energy will have a dramatic effect on us and the people we interact with in ways that have to be experienced to be believed – it's that incredible.

63

P A I N   &   D I S E A S E

Pain and disease quite often walk hand in hand. Pain and disease can come from physical ailments or from deep within our consciousness. It's helpful to understand the dynamics of pain in the physical body. Even more important is understanding the dynamics of pain in your feeling body (your thoughts and your feelings). Pain, both physical and emotional, can start as a mild dis-ease and increase until it manifests as pain, or it can hit you like a Mack truck. Being hit by a sudden loss or being confronted with an unexpected burden can literally knock the wind out of you and put you into a state of shock. Realize that pain is most intense when you are closest to it. So, how can we separate ourselves from this pain? Pain pills and anti-depressants only help numb the effects and disconnect you from yourself, sapping your conscious energy, hindering your ability to address the actual cause of the pain.

The truth is that when you self-center your conscious energy on what is causing you pain, you move closer to it, causing yet more intense pain. The answer is to consciously move away from the pain by becoming an observer. The simple act of observation shifts your focus from the tree (you and your pain) to the forest (that which supports and sustains the tree).

Start asking yourself questions: what hurts? How is the pain affecting my physical body? How is the pain affecting my thinking body? How is the pain affecting my feeling body? As you start questioning and looking for answers, you will notice your conscious energy begins to shift and your focus will realign from being self-centered to becoming more selflessly centered. You will move away from your pain and into a conscious realm of clarity, where suffering has purpose — the reward of conscious growth and the understanding that comes with that growth.

Disease is a state of imbalance that manifests physically in the part of the body associated with the imbalance. Quite often this disease is in part brought on by abuse or neglect of the physical body. Without exception, the disease is always supported by an imbalance of the conscious energy that is truly you. If disease goes unchecked for too long, pain will bring the imbalance of the disease to your attention.

When doctors treat their diseased patients, whether or not they know it, they are trying to balance the imbalance in their patient's body. Too often doctors treat the physical symptoms while overlooking the energy supporting the disease. When medical science finds this truth and starts looking for the energy imbalances that support the disease, it will discover numerous cures that have until now remained elusive.

Once we understand that we are eternal beings clothed in physical bodies, we begin to grasp that our feeling bodies (our emotions) are here to keep us in touch with the realities we are creating. When your energy is flowing on its natural course, supported by the matrix that is your unique energy given to you at the moment of your birth into physical manifestation, you feel a sense of ease, a sense of joy, a sense of oneness with an energy greater than you. When we allow our focus to shift away from our supporting energy (our higher self, Christ consciousness) and become focused on our Ego's energy (self-centered energy), the imbalance that is created by our misdirected energy creates dis-ease, which can manifest as physical disease if not corrected.

Dis-ease is an imbalance of conscious energy; physical disease is an imbalance of conscious energy that has settled into the physical realm from the conscious realm of thought and feeling. Disease needs consciousness (thought and feeling) in order for disease to exist and grow. We age and ail because our thoughts and feelings support the process, but in actuality, our bodies are designed to function for thousands of years if properly maintained physically and consciously. Science knows that the body is continually replenishing itself, but in our ignorance, we keep sending our physical bodies conscious energy (thoughts and feelings) that stimulates old age and disease. Entertaining thoughts and feelings that tell us that our bodies are supposed to grow old and weak with age supports the aging process.

Knock it off! You are better than that. You are God, and God is greater. You are a Creator, created in God's exact conscious image. You are supported by All that is (God) and your path to perfection has already been created; you are already there. Your view is just obscured by all the poop you have been sloshing around in. Dis-ease and poop are a lot alike: both are designed to help things grow, but neither one was meant to be used as a carpet or an easy chair. Standing in it only stinks and draws flies.

64

THE CHICKEN AND THE EGG

What came first, the chicken or the egg? Seen from the perspective of the created, it seems impossible to understand, but turn your perspective from that of the created to that of the Creator and the answer is rather straightforward.

In order to bring anything into manifestation, you first start with a desire or need for that which is to be brought forth. This desire or need helps to define the properties of that which is to be brought forth, such as what its purpose is and how best to express itself. It is after the defined properties of that which is to be manifested have been consciously realized (the chicken) that the conscious understanding of the desire (the chicken) can be blended with the joy of having that which is desired (the chicken), creating the vibrational matrix that will bring forth the object of desire (the chicken). Simply put, the chicken, or that which is to be brought forth into manifestation, is created first, consciously. The conscious understanding of that which is to be manifested (the chicken) can now be blended with the feelings of joy and excitement that come with having that which is desired (the chicken).

The outgoing positively charged desire defined (the thought) for the chicken blends with the receptive negatively charged energy of the wish fulfilled (the joy of having the chicken), creating a vibrational matrix (a mini-"Big Bang") that guides and supports the necessary matter to bring forth the egg that evolves into the chicken. Simply put, the chicken came first consciously, which created the matrix necessary to bring forth the egg which becomes the chicken.

65

SIMPLE TRUTHS THAT WILL HELP IN UNDERSTANDING THE THEORY OF ALMOST EVERYTHING

1. Infinite energy - The very first tick of energy ever expressed was non-physical, vibrating at a frequency lighter (finer) than can be measured physically. Infinite energy transcends time and space and is the eternal energy that animates this finite realm.

2. Relative dynamics - Relative dynamics is the interaction between two polar opposites: positive and negative, outgoing and receptive. Relative dynamics is the force that animates creation from the creative infinite conscious awareness (thought and feeling) that guides and observes creation, to the finite expressions that make up our physical reality. The electrical force that powers all of creation is the one force (God, singularity) separated into its two polar opposites: (+) positive outgoing energy and (-) negative receptive grounding energy. This dynamic can be easily understood by observing electricity and its effects on finite matter as it animates everything in existence.

Everything in existence is an expression of the one force (God, singularity) and it is the relative separation of the qualities of everything in existence that allows the one force to be defined in a multitude of expression and supplies the energy to animate all that is in existence.

3. The matrix – Creation is based on the desire to create, which is receptive in nature (-), and the definition of that desire (+) defined in its state of completion, which is much like a blueprint. To understand the dynamics involved in creation, science must realize that everything in existence came from a non-physical infinite source, or no thing. The vibrational frequencies that define everything from physical light to

the heaviest, densest matter can be measured and weighed, elucidating physical matter's molecular makeup allowing for understanding of the infinite energy expressing it.

The infinite non-physical force that supports our finite physical realm also has various frequencies that range from very high, and beyond most people's ability to comprehend, to a vibrational frequency that rests just above finite matter's vibrational rate. The vibrational rate of everything in existence is what defines and separates everything in existence. The threshold between infinite and finite is determined by vibrational frequency and anything vibrating at a frequency higher than that threshold is infinite and non-physical. Anything vibrating below that threshold can be witnessed as physical and finite (temporary).

While science can't measure this lower infinite energy, it can measure its effects on finite matter. The matrix that acts as the infinite foundation that finite matter requires to be expressed in the myriad of ways that make up the physical universe is multi-dimensional with varying frequencies that support the multitude of finite expressions ranging from light to the densest of matter. Everything comes from the same source, and it is the vibrational frequency supporting finite matter that gives finite matter its unique characteristics. This matrix is the very first energy that initiates creation and, being infinite in nature, is expressed instantaneously in the moment, unaffected by the parameters imposed upon finite matter by time and space.

The matrix is the link between the infinite force and the finite expression. The energy and the information that define our current finite state of expression (there have been countless) came from the refined energy and information from the finite expression that preceded it, which was powered by the energy and information from the one before it. This is how conscious awareness (which we call God) has evolved from very simple beginnings to the complexity that is our current reality.

What science calls the "Big Bang" is a natural effect that comes from the self-evident energy and information that preceded it. The available information that has been expressed, defined, and refined in the previous "Big Bang" creates the matrix, or blueprint, that supports the current finite expression. This finite realm exists as a means to express, define, and refine infinite conscious awareness, and it is the information and infinite energy that comes from the experience that remains and records the vibrational information and energy that can be expressed in ever grander expressions, leading to a greater understanding of the creative dynamics involved and ultimately the evolution of the creative force. Once the finite expression has served its purpose, it is recycled as information and energy back up into the higher vibrational frequency of the infinite source (force) that expressed it. The finite realm, as the word "finite" implies, is a temporary expression that ceases to exist once it has served its purpose.

The matrix is the first energy expressed in a "Big Bang" and is the last energy left after the finite matter is refined; it is the informational energy that initiates the next "Big Bang." Everything that has ever existed and ever will exist is conscious energy. The diversity we see in creation is this myriad of vibrational frequencies that allow for the most effective means to gain conscious evolution of the one force. Energy comes from the one infinite force (God) and gets expressed into its highest potential expression as the matrix (blueprint).

What science calls black holes are the portals that link the infinite creative force (God) with the finite expression (physical reality) and act as a two-way link between the infinite creative force (God) and the created finite realm, allowing for the exchange of conscious information and energy. This finite realm comes from the one force (God), which science calls the singularity, and is expressed first as non-physical energy (the matrix), creating the foundation that attracts the various components necessary for the creation of this finite realm. The matrix is the blueprint and comes into being with all the information necessary to facilitate creation. Infinite energy is brought into existence through black holes and lowered into finite expression first as light forming to the matrix as the various suns in our universe, after which it can be "lowered into" hydrogen, helium, and the heavier elements, which are then attracted by the matrix to make up what we see as our finite reality.

The matrix attracts the necessary specific matter that makes up the multitude of physical, finite forms that comprise our universe. The size and character of each galaxy, sun, and planet is determined by the matrix. It is the matrix that distorts space, causing light to bend around the matrix that supports the suns and planets in the universe. Gravity attracts physical matter, causing the matrix to be distorted to accommodate the mass. Once the suns or planets have reached their pre-determined mass, the matrix stops accepting incoming matter, much like a glass becoming full, ensuring that the universe gets constructed according to the pre-determined parameters set forth at the time of the "Big Bang." The relative dynamics involved in the creation of this physical realm attracts the appropriate matter to the matrix. This attracting force is called gravity. Its polar opposite is what causes light to bend around the planetary bodies and is the cradle that supports the placement and movement of everything in the universe. In short, gravity and the matrix are two relative aspects of the same force. Gravity attracts the necessary matter and the matrix defines and supports its expression and movement.

4. Time and space – Time and space originally came into being as the result of infinite energy's frequency being lowered into what has become finite matter. Infinite energy's frequency vibrates at a rate finer than physical matter and does not create the vibrational distortions that require time and space to define it. What is seen as a finite expression is a defined distortion in the infinite matrix that will eventually return to its natural higher infinite frequency, giving the finite expression defined characteristics and shelf-life. Time and space were the result of infinite energy being lowered in frequency to the point that it created a temporary vibrational expression of energy that distorted the higher frequency of the force originating it.

The higher frequencies of the infinite force (God, singularity) have a natural rhythm that is defined and constant and the distortions in the fabric of this matrix create what we experience as our finite reality. These distortions always get rebalanced up into the higher infinite frequencies that they were generated from and it is this interaction of infinite and finite vibrational energy that allows for the infinite force to expand its frequencies as the finite distortions are incorporated into the higher infinite frequencies that generated it.

This distortion in the infinite force created a temporary, finite tick that could be observed by the force originating it. The lower frequency created a point of reference, and the distortion it created was defined by the ripples the energy created, bringing into existence the space in between the ripples necessary to define the event. Time defined the energy's temporary expression into the lower frequency of finite matter and its return back up into the higher infinite realm of the creative force. Time and space were a natural occurrence that became self-evident when infinite conscious energy was lowered into a temporary finite state of expression. Time and space are the means that the infinite creative force uses to express, define, and refine conscious energy, allowing for the evolution of conscious awareness (understanding).

5. Inflation – Science's explanation for how the initial burst of energy exceeded the speed of light is what they call inflation. Science knows that the "Big Bang" exceeded the speed of light but is yet to understand the dynamics involved. What has eluded science is the fact that this finite physical realm came from and is powered by an infinite force (God). This force is non-physical, transcends time and space, and is not limited by the physical, temporo-spatial parameters of finite matter. In Genesis, light was created twice. The first light was infinite, non-physical, and occurred instantaneously in the moment prior to the second physical finite light, bringing with it time and space and the parameters that time and space impose on finite matter. It's helpful to know that creation always occurs in the moment. The parameters time and space impose upon finite matter give the creative force the means to better understand the creative process, but the creative force is not limited to the dynamics imposed by time and space, as can be seen in the beginning and explains how inflation broke the speed of light.

6. Black holes – Black holes are the portals that link the infinite force (God) to this finite realm. The infinite energy that governs and powers this finite realm comes into finite existence through black

holes and refined finite energy becomes infinite again once it has been raised back up into the higher frequencies of infinite energy where it can return to the source that originated it. Physical matter that vibrates at the lower levels of finite expression do not come, or go through, black holes. This is why science can't see into them. There is no thing to see because black holes are the portals that link this finite physical realm to the infinite, non-physical force.

7. Electromagnetism – As everything is relative, there are always two sides to everything that gets expressed into finite existence. Likewise, electromagnetism has two defined properties – attraction and repulsion. Electromagnetism is an aspect of the matrix that balances the infinite energy that supports creation, attracts to the blueprint of the matrix the raw materials that make up this finite realm, and repels materials that don't fit where they don't belong. The two forces in balance [(+) and (-)] create the neutral buoyancy in space that allows finite matter (planets, suns, galaxies) to move through space with precision. The attractive side of electromagnetism binds everything in existence and creates what we experience as gravity, while the repulsive side distorts space, causing light to bend around the matrix that surrounds, defines, and supports finite matter. The neutral balance of electromagnetism is what defines empty space, allowing finite matter to move through it without matter accumulating in locations that are not defined, in perfect accord with the blueprint of the matrix. Electromagnetism is one relative aspect of the infinite energy of the matrix, as is gravity, the strong, and the weak force.

8. Gravity - Gravity is the result of the attractive side of electromagnetism and its effects and strength on physical finite matter is determined by the amount and balance of polarity of the electromagnetic force in the matrix. This in turn dictates the character, position and movement of the various planets, suns, galaxies, and everything in the universe in accordance with the blueprint of the matrix. Gravity, like all forces, is an aspect of the infinite energy that defines and supports creation.

9. Weak and strong force – All things being relative, the strong and weak force are two aspects of the same force, which is the matrix

(blueprint) that creation rests upon. Gravity and electromagnetism, the strong and weak forces, along with dark energy and dark matter are all aspects of this one creative force. You can't have construction without its polar opposite, deconstruction. The strong force is the attractive, constructive side of electromagnetism that attracts the necessary elements according to the defined blueprint of the matrix for the creation of everything in our universe. The weak force is its relative opposite, supporting defined finite matter to be recycled once it has served its purpose and allowing the energy to be utilized over and over in the creative process. Nothing is static and everything in finite existence is always undergoing a process of creation and growth or deterioration and recycling. These two forces support this process and are relative aspects of the one creative force.

10. Dark energy – Dark energy is the infinite energy that powers everything in this finite realm. Science can detect its effects on finite matter but can't find the energy itself (hence the name dark energy) because it is infinite in nature and vibrates at a rate too fine to be detected physically. Science's inability to find this energy comes from a misaligned perspective on creation. The creative force is infinite and non-physical and cannot be weighed and measured like finite matter can. Once science figures out this simple truth we will step into a whole new understanding of creation and the dynamics that support it.

Everything in existence comes from the same source and gets defined according to its vibrational frequency. Finite matter, physical light to lead vibrates at frequencies that define them in a manner that can be weighed and measured allowing for the study of the effects that come from their interaction, allowing for understanding to be gained in the dynamics involved. The force that creates, guides and supports the expressions of this finite realm is infinite, non-physical, and vibrates at a rate that can't be measured physically. Dark energy comes and goes through black holes (finite matter cannot enter black holes because its lower frequencies do not allow it to do so). Its effects can be found everywhere in the universe, empty space included, energizing and animating finite matter.

11. Dark matter – It is important to remember that this finite realm is an expression of infinite conscious energy. The infinite conscious energy that supports and animates this finite realm has always existed, will always exist, and transcends time and space. The matrix that links finite creation to the infinite creative force is comprised of the four elements conventionally called electromagnetism, gravity, and the weak and strong forces. Dark energy and dark matter are also aspects of the matrix that support and animate this finite realm. While dark energy energizes and animates finite matter, dark matter acts as the infinite substance, allowing physical matter to form into the various elements that make up the finite realm we exist in.

Dark matter supports light being light; the universe in all its multitude of expressions being galaxies, suns, and planets, down to the most minuscule particle. It is dark matter that binds our physical bodies, supporting and keeping the multitude of atoms that give our physical bodies their molecular structure and the proper alignment and allowing all the components vibrating at various frequencies in each and every body to be expressed. This is what gives every thing its unique identity. Dark matter acts as the negative (the film) in the matrix that attracts the necessary finite matter needed to express the defined energy of the negative creating finite matter (the picture). Dark matter is infinite, non-physical, and cannot be measured physically. Its effects on physical matter can.

66

T H E O R Y   O F   A L M O S T
E V E R Y T H I N G
–   T H E   B A S I C S   –

Science has for a long time struggled to come up with a comprehensive theory that would explain the dynamics involved in creation. The problem lies not with the available information (which is abundant) but with science's perspective. Viewing our complex reality from the superficial perspective of the created inhibits science's understanding. Science can detect some of the energy (information) being expressed but can't see through the finite expression of creation to get to the source expressing it. They can see the effects of this energy on physical matter but are unable to understand the dynamics involved.

Science continues to wrestle with the thorny question of how "something" could come from "nothing" – how to reconcile how this finite physical realm could have started from a state where no thing existed. Getting some thing from no thing seems impossible from the perspective of the created. Where did the substance and energy necessary to power the event come from, and what directed it? Solving this conundrum requires a different understanding of creation, 180 degrees from science's present perspective: the perspective of the Creator.

First, the eternal state of selfless awareness must be understood. What has always existed and transcends time and space is selfless awareness, a state of infinite conscious receptivity that has always been aware but had no thing to be aware of. Think of this state of existence as a conscious matrix with a fixed vibrational signature, lacking a point of reference – awareness with no thing to be aware of. So, what was the event that began existence that eventually unfolded into the reality we experience now? The initial spark that created the point of reference (God's I am) that began this great Adventure developed when the state of selfless awareness turned in on itself. (God's I am was established when the truth of that first event became self-evident.) This event established the basic dynamics that creation rides upon. Separation was established between the selfless state of Creation's self-center, allowing for the interaction of the very first polar opposites: selfless awareness (unfocused energy) and the lower vibrational energy of self-centered awareness (focused energy). That initial spark, as insignificant as it was, established a wealth of information. It established a point of reference (God's I am) based upon separation and the interaction of polar opposites. Self-evident truth gave way to God's understanding, which in turn eventually gave way to our present reality.

Simply put, the energy that has always existed has a frequency. The very first "Big Bang" occurred when a void separated the two polar extremes of that frequency, defining their opposing properties: positive, outgoing and negative, receptive energy. The void created the separation of the positive and negative aspects of the energy defining the properties, and the collision of the two polar opposites returning to their prior state of expression created the very first "Big Bang," which in turn created another slightly larger void (gap), repeating the process. Each subsequent "Big Bang" was the result of the one that preceded it.

There have been countless "Big Bangs", and each new expression has brought with it the evidence of the truth behind that expression, which has continually led to greater understanding and growth. The truth that becomes self-evident with each and every expression that results from the relative interaction of polar opposites is the fuel (information and expressed energy) that facilitates the evolution of the force (source) expressing it. This is how no thing has been able to evolve into the omnipotent, omnipresent intelligence that is self-evident as ourselves and all of creation. Everything that exists comes from the same source and is interconnected. What differentiates light from lead is the vibrational rate of energy that expresses it. The first expression was a mere conscious tick of energy, not physical and barely recognizable. But that small vibrational variance created a great deal of information. As each expression came into being, the self-evident dynamics involved laid the foundation of understanding for the next.

Evolution has brought us to this point, and evolution has, from the very beginning, been consciously guided by a creative force (God). This creative force is infinite and exists (vibrates) in the higher non-physical realm of creation. What we experience as our finite reality is this infinite force being expressed at a lower vibrational level.

Everything is interconnected, and it is each aspect of defined creation's unique vibration that allows the one force to be expressed in a myriad of ways, defining everything from light to lead, supporting everything's unique character, giving rise to the complexity of the universe. The infinite and the finite are one and the same, two sides of the same coin, with the infinite being the source and the finite being the expression. What science is calling dark energy is in fact light, light that vibrates at a rate finer than that which can be measured in this finite realm of expression. That is why science can measure its effects on physical matter but can't measure the force itself.

But how did this non-physical force become physical? The polarity of the eternal state that has always existed is receptive in nature, (-). The first spark that started the process was its polar opposite, outgoing and (+). The reaction or interaction of these two poles created the relative dynamic that powers existence and the interaction made it self-evident that there was a point of reference and energy being expressed. This dynamic has supported the evolution of the basic conscious awareness that at first was a small tick of energy into a state of self-awareness that is the infinite force expressing what science sees as our finite universe. The self-evident information that has resulted from each relative interaction is the dynamic that has, from the very beginning, supported the evolution of infinite awareness (God). Allowing for the countless expressions of that force has brought into finite manifestation what we are experiencing as our universe. This energy was infinite in nature, with its vibrational frequency moving at a finer rate than can be measured physically. This energy is, and has always been, expressed in the moment and transcends time and space. A great deal of effort (time was yet to be defined) was invested in understanding this energy by the self-aware force (God), learning how to manipulate its vibrational frequency, by raising and lowering its expression.

Time and space also became self-evident, with the finite expression requiring space to define its properties and time to define its movement in and out of finite expression. The relative dance between Creator and created began with this simple event and has led to the synchronistic complexity we are now experiencing as our reality.

67

THEORY OF ALMOST EVERYTHING
– GOD'S ETERNAL ENGINE –

Understanding the dynamics involved in creation and the force that animates the process is essential for coming up with a theory that explains the synchronicity we can see in this finite realm we call reality.

The first question would be: Where did the energy that brought about the "Big Bang" come from and what is its nature? Simply put, the energy that kick-started our present reality came from the "Big Bang" that preceded it. This energy is infinite (non-physical) and possesses a vibrational frequency higher than can be measured in this physical finite realm. This energy contained all the information that the "Big Bang" that preceded it expressed, defined, and refined from the finite interaction of infinite conscious energy during its expression. Creation begins at the highest level of expression, which is infinite, and, once it manifests physically, works its way down in frequency starting with the matrix (blueprint) that finite creation rides upon. This matrix contains the energy and information necessary to support the creative process, is multi-dimensional, and attracts the appropriate elements that make up our reality.

The first light was non-physical and transcended time and space. The second light came not from one location but through this multitude of established portals in the matrix (black holes). This second light was finite and established time and space. Built into the structure of the matrix are variables that allow a certain amount of flexibility in the evolution of creation as it unfolds, always elevating creation to its highest expression. This variable can be found within the binary code, allowing the creative force to adjust to the infinite energy that supports this finite realm as time and space move the creative mechanism as our finite reality unfolds. The flexibility built into the binary code that defines finite reality allows for adjustments in the supportive infinite matrix that is the fabric that our finite realm is supported by. This flexibility allows an infinite force that is all knowing to gain new understanding supporting the evolution of infinite conscious understanding. The binary code was the creative force's (God's) first means of expression and is the code that the creative force uses to define creation. The flexibility that this code supports allows for the refinement and evolution of infinite understanding.

Once the current information and energy has reached its optimal expression, expansion is reversed into contraction and the universe begins refining its informational energy. Where in the beginning light came first, with the heavier elements coming into expression as the vibrational frequency was lowered, the opposite is true with the ending of the finite reality that preceded this current one, with the heavier elements being processed first and light being the last finite element to be processed.

The energy and information required to create what science calls the "Big Bang" came from the "Big Bang" that preceded it. The universe's initial burst into existence began at the higher infinite frequencies that transcend time and space and occurred in the moment. Creation always occurs in the moment. The future and the past are mere points of reference that help to define creation, but creation always occurs in the moment. The singularity from which, according to science, creation is generated is infinite and transcends time and space. Finite matter is an expression of infinite conscious energy and exists as a means to express conscious energy, define that energy, and refine it to its highest, most pure expression. In other words, this finite realm is an illusion with purpose, which is to express, define, and refine conscious energy. Once the finite expression has served its purpose, it gets refined back into the infinite vibrational frequency that originated it, making way and powering the next expression.

What science is calling inflation and the fact that the initial burst produced by the "Big Bang" exceeded the speed of light can be explained knowing that the first energy that brought forth our present finite state was infinite and vibrated at a non-physical frequency unfettered by the limitations of finite matter. Inflation occurred in the eternal moment and was instantaneous, and it was not until infinite energy was lowered in frequency, creating physical light, that finite matter assumed the parameters that circumscribe and define it. The infinite energy that defines and animates this finite realm does so in what can be called the eternal moment. Everything that has ever been created and ever will be created is always created and supported in this eternal moment.

The initial burst of energy (it was not an explosion) was non-physical, vibrating at a frequency finer than finite matter. Its outward projection into what became the matrix was instantaneous, creating the blueprint and points of entry for infinite energy and information to be lowered first into physical light, and then hydrogen and helium and the heavier elements. When the frequency of infinite energy was lowered to the point that physical light became expressed, time and space came into being as the result of that expression with black holes acting as portals to bring infinite energy to be lowered in frequency, first as physical light that formed to the points in the matrix that defined and supported the creation of the suns throughout the universe, which then began the process of lowering energy further down into the heavier elements.

The "Big Bang" was brought forth and was energized with all the infinite information and energy that came from the one preceding it and this fact can account for the tremendous amount of energy necessary to initiate the process. The initial burst of infinite energy carried with it all the information necessary to define this finite state in its perfect state of completion. This non-physical infinite energy is the matrix or blueprint that our physical finite reality rides on and is the reason that the movement of the cosmos (universe) is so predictable. The matrix links the infinite creative energy that defines and supports creation with this finite created reality.

The sun is not burning hydrogen and helium, it is *producing* them. Infinite energy comes through the black holes in each galaxy to the suns, where it is brought down vibrationally into the finite physical realm as light, then hydrogen and helium, and further down the vibrational scale of creation into the heavier elements. Creation comes from a singularity, where a blending of positive conscious energy (defined desired creation based on the self-evident information that had preceded it) interacts with receptive grounding energy, creating a vibrational composite of the two energies' combined forces, producing a matrix that, while still infinite and non-physical, vibrated at a lower rate just above what can be measured as physical finite matter, connecting the creation with the creative force. The matrix is the blueprint generated from the informational energy from the "Big Bang" that preceded it that attracts the necessary elements as they are created and brought into their defined physical vibrational expression. It is the matrix that gives matter its identity and supports its expression and evolution into its highest expression. The positioning and defined orbits of the galaxies, and each and every star and planet in the universe, is set in this matrix and allows for the interaction of energy as gravity pushes and pulls on physical matter, producing the energy that supports and fuels this reality.

The infinite, non-physical energy of the matrix makes it possible for gravity to do what gravity does, without pulling all physical matter in on itself. In essence, the universe is one big engine powering the expression of conscious energy, allowing for a greater quantity of information (knowledge) that propels the eternal process of growth.

A small example of this engine is our planet. Earth has all of the elements of an electric motor/generator: a metal core wrapped in a magnetic field. The earth's movement, just like everything in the universe, is powered electronically, not mechanically. The precision of the mechanics of the earth, our solar system, and the universe would be impossible using mere physical mechanics. The matrix's electromagnetic forces attracted the necessary elements as their vibrational identity became established and acts as the foundation of creation, maintaining and guiding creation to its ultimate expression.

The universe, and all the elements that make up the multitude of galaxies and planets rests upon the electromagnetic grid of the matrix, which links the point of creation (the creative force) to the defined creation at its point of completion (the blueprint is always of the finished product.) What we see as the movement of the cosmos, with all the energy being expressed, is creation under construction, moving in a timely manner governed by the defined parameters of time and space towards its defined outcome (the finished product as guided by the matrix or blueprint).

Rather impressively, the dynamics supporting this complex process allows for energy to become expressed in unanticipated ways, making self-evident new discoveries and facilitating evolution of conscious creative energy. What looks like chaos in the universe is relative dynamics powering the process of creation. You can't have creation without a certain amount of chaos – it's part of the relative process.

Reconciling the theory of the very small with the theory of the very large becomes fairly easy once science comes to understand that all the small, non-physical energy that powers the universe is infinite and transcends time and space. Creation has always occurred in the moment. From the very beginning to this exact moment, every thought, action, and manifestation have always occurred in the moment. As time and space move finite matter across the infinite eternal moment of creation, the relative dynamics involved can be observed and understood better because of the separation that space allows for and the timely expression that time supports. It is the relative exchange of energy between infinite and finite, Creator and created that define all that is.

Space acts as the canvas that supports the expression of finite matter and time acts as creation's paint brush, supporting the movement and evolution of finite matter and allowing the infinite force to gain understanding as to the effects it has on finite matter. The creative force defines creation and it is creation that defines the creative force. What science sees as dark matter, dark energy, and the four forces are all aspects of the one creative force, forming the infinite structure that supports, guides, and animates our physical universe. Think of the universe as a small baby when it came into being, with the matrix supporting it at a fraction of the size it will eventually grow to. As the universe expanded, new black holes came into being, which created more suns which produced more hydrogen and helium as well as heavier elements that enlarge the mass of the universe as the matrix expands itself.

When the universe expands to the farthest point of the defined blueprint of the matrix as set forth at the instance of the "Big Bang," contraction begins and the process of refinement of all the finite matter that has been brought into expression begins with the heaviest elements being refined first, leading to the finite universes eventual return to the lighter elements and ultimately back into infinite energy and information where it returns to the force that originated it through black holes initiating the next "Big Bang." The growth of each universe – supported by each matrix that brings it into being – supports the growth and evolution of the infinite conscious force that generates it, with each new "Big Bang" expanding in energy, size, and complexity. This process has supported the evolution of the creative force from a state of no thingness to the complexity of our present reality. But even the reality that we observe is but a glimmer of all that truly exists along myriad levels of expression, infinite and finite.

DAILY EXERCISES SUPPORTING CONSCIOUS EVOLUTION

Knowledge is a powerful tool. Knowledge put into practice is a path to mastery. Investing daily time and effort in practicing the art of refinement will lead to accelerated growth and the enlightenment that comes with refining one's consciousness.

Below is a list of simple exercises that will help in the process of refining your consciousness and strengthening your connection to God and the Creative Force.

1. Take time every day to turn your attention inward and focus on how the energy (your thoughts and feelings) is affecting your body, making adjustments to raise the energy to a more joyful, loving expression.

2. Make the effort, several times each day, to focus your conscious attention in the moment on what is occurring around you. This may sound foolish, but pay attention to how little time we spend in the moment we are in. Much of our conscious attention is focused outside ourselves, thinking about what occurred in the past (five minutes ago, yesterday, and last year) and anticipating what is about to occur (in the next five minutes, tomorrow, or next year.) Our lives always occur in the moment. Learning to spend more time focused on this eternal moment strengthens our creative powers.

3. Practice the art of listening. Understanding other people's perspectives requires that we stop generating thoughts and feelings and openly receive the information (energy) being expressed by others without thinking of our next response while the other person is still talking. Remember that we learn by listening, not talking.

4. Practice the art of giving more than you take. Giving to others in need, whether that need be physical, mental, emotional, or spiritual, lifts up the person and also raises your conscious energy to a higher, more loving level.

5. Take time each day to audit the events of that day and their effects on your conscious feeling body, allowing you to raise the energy you invest in your daily life.

6. Two very special times in our day are when we first wake and just before we drift off to sleep. Our minds are at rest and more receptive to the conscious flow of infinite intelligence coming from the Creative Force (God). At night, before falling asleep, take the time to visualize that which you desire in its state of completion and feel the excitement of the wish fulfilled as you fall asleep. Be careful what you wish for because this is a powerful creative tool that will bring results. You are co-creating with God and the Creative Force – create wisely!

   When you first wake, take time to become aware of the wisdom that you received while your body and ego rested. It is at night, while our egos have relinquished control of our consciousness, that we receive much of the wisdom from that greater part of who we are (God) that can guide us into the higher, more joyous and productive expressions of self.

7. As the events of our daily lives unfold and we find ourselves in challenging situations and interactions with others, learn to quietly ask the question "How does this serve me?" This simple act will shift control from the ego up into your higher conscious awareness raising the energy to a more positive level.

8. Practice feeling joyous, loving thoughts of gratitude as often during your day as possible. This will help to raise your energy up into the higher creative realm, effecting you and those you interact with in a positive manner.

9. We all seem to have memories of negative events in our lives that we cling to despite the unpleasant effects they have on our conscious feeling bodies. An effective exercise that can aid in releasing these negative memories is taking a piece of paper, folding it in half, labeling one side positive and uplifting, and the other side negative and painful. Start listing all the different aspects of the event causing the memories, assigning each aspect to the proper side of the paper. As you break down and categorize the different aspects of the memory, you will become aware of the different ingredients making up your memory.

Breaking down and categorizing the various ingredients making up your memory will allow you to observe the effects that memory is having on you right now in the moment, making it easier to understand and release the thoughts and feelings that are not in your best interest. We are meant to live in the moment where creation is always occurring, right here, right now. Our memories are incredible tools helping to define who we are, giving each of us defined points of reference in our lives. We are not meant to cling to the memories that lower our vibrational energy. The negative events in our lives help to give us the relative information that allows us to define the quality of our lives. Remember, you can't have "good" unless you have "not good" to help define it. Our experiences broaden our understanding, but we must learn to release the emotional baggage that does not serve our highest expression of self.

This simple exercise will help in maintaining a light, joyous, childlike view of life, rather than a childish, emotionally heavy life limited by self-imposed negativity. It's all relative, and our power lies in how we choose to focus and express our conscious energy.

We are always growing. The question is, how do you choose to grow: stronger or weaker? Smarter and open-minded, or small-minded and opinionated? Are you emotionally open and available for what life brings you or closed and afraid of what is coming? It's all about perspective and where you choose to focus your conscious energy.

Make a point to invest time on a daily basis to exercise your physical body and your intellect, and clarify the emotional energy you take in as you experience the events of your daily life. Live a life consciously connected to the person within your body and maintain a conscious awareness of the energy that comes from within you. Remember, we never stop growing.

EPILOGUE

We are living in a watershed moment in our evolution as infinite children of God. God's infinite energy has, for some time, supported our self-centered expression, giving us a more defined sense of self and strengthening each of our individual identities. The polarity of the energy that has been supporting us has been thought (+) grounded in intuition (-). The December 21, 2012 date, an important date on the Mayan calendar that was widely feared to mark the end of the world, instead marked the end of a cycle that has supported our journey into self-centered expression. The energy has begun to shift its polarity back to intuition (-) grounded in intellect (+), while the cycle we are now leaving supports our self-centered understanding and has been moving us away from the state of innocence we began with (thought is outgoing). The shift in energy is now supporting our return to conscious oneness with God and the infinite energy that is who we truly are.

The turmoil that comes from people's unease with this shift in conscious energy is evident worldwide. The nightly news reflects this unease felt around the world at this time. Those oriented to their lower self-centered conscious energy are reacting in a beast-like manner as the energy shifts and begins to draw the more selfless among us into a more intuitive (receptive) inward relationship with ourselves and God.

As the self-centered ride the inertia of their lower energy, they will feel greater separation from the energy that supports us and the relative Adventure, and will behave accordingly. Those who are more selfless in nature will be drawn within to receive the wisdom necessary to bring the suffering we are all experiencing to its most fruitful conclusion. Remember, we are here to learn and grow from the lessons that life brings us. We are living through a very special time, a time of harvest that requires that we become mindful of ourselves, our surroundings, and the blessings that come with this incredible moment. Taking the time in our daily lives to be still, turn our attention inward, and become aware of the energy that animates our lives will enable us to take full advantage of this incredible time in our evolution.

We are born with the light of God. That is who we truly are. It is this light of God that calls to all of us, and that which brought me to write this simple book. Like many, I spent much time and effort seeking this light outside myself until God finally slapped me upside the head and let me know it was time to stop looking for something outside myself that I always possessed within.

This book is not a product of my intellect. It was given to me intuitively. Over the eleven years that it took to complete, I experienced the process of exercising aspects of ego that impeded the flow of God's selfless energy which brought God's wisdom to these pages. Through it all, I endured moments that were quite uncomfortable, sometimes downright frightening, as I clung to my selfish identity. But eventually I was shown that as I released my selfish need to control my environment according to the limited information my ego had allowed me to see, I gained access to an energy greater than myself and the strength and wisdom that comes with it, empowering me to handle anything and everything that life could throw at me.

While there have been many challenges, many of which seemed insurmountable, I always felt in my heart God's sustaining light energizing and guiding the process. Every time I got off track, I was gently nudged back into the light. I have been required to put these truths in this book into practice in my life. It hasn't always been pretty, but I know from experience that it is doable.

While my foundation has been set on the life and teachings of Jesus, I know that following the teachings of Muhammad, the Buddha, and all great masters will bring you to your truth because the same truth runs through all true faiths; the only difference is that each possesses its own unique perspective on the one truth.

Understanding the truths of these other great faiths has made me a better, more understanding Christian, and I am grateful for the wisdom I have gained.

We are experiencing the chaos that comes with construction. In order for this golden age to emerge, we must first tear down the self-centered structure that permeates our reality. The most selfish among us are clinging to the finite structures that are causing all the imbalances we are now seeing in the world. They lack the wisdom to see beyond their own self-centered agenda to understand the revolutionary shift in energy taking hold.

God supports our awakening, and the most selfless among us are being drawn within to receive the necessary guidance. Know that God is right here, right now, supporting you and your journey into self-awareness as a child of God. I don't have words to express the joy, gratitude, and excitement for what we are about to receive. We are standing in a very special moment in our evolution. Those of us who are ready are now experiencing a shift in our consciousness, drawing our attention away from the distractions of the superficial world and toward an inward intuitive connection with ourselves, each other, and God, preparing us for the golden age that is almost upon us.

As more individuals find their inner connection to God, energy is building and approaching a tipping point. The story of the hundredth monkey will help to explain the dynamics involved where those who possess this selfless connection to God will begin to experience what is known as the Rapture. This doesn't involve God beaming us up and out of here (we would miss all the benefits of this incredible transformation), but rather the elevation of our conscious awareness to the level of the Creator, where we can find transcendence in the boundless wisdom and support of God. Now, we must stay in the moment, pay attention, and look beyond ourselves to find our true center within. Let go and let God.

Things are getting hectic around the world; there is always a certain amount of chaos with construction as old structures (self-centered values) get torn down to make way for something better. We are in the midst of a major remodel of our very existence. While a bit inconvenient, the new structure will be beautiful beyond words. Everything you need to get the most out of this transformation lies within you. God has supplied you with everything needed and is right here, right now, supporting you in this very special moment.

I am excited for us! We are ready for this. Everything is in place to support our step back into conscious oneness with God and All that is. The time is right and we have the support of God, our Angels, and the mechanics of creation. Our success is a done deal. That's God's promise to us, and God always keeps God's word.

Love and Light,
Your Brother,
Greg J. Royal

www.ingramcontent.com/pod-product-compliance
Lightning Source LLC
LaVergne TN
LVHW051509080426
835509LV00017B/1997